# HEALING
*with the*
# ANGELS

## Also by Doreen Virtue, Ph.D.

*MANIFESTING WITH THE ANGELS*
*KARMA RELEASING*
*HEALING YOUR APPETITE, HEALING YOUR LIFE*
*HEALING WITH THE ANGELS*
*DIVINE GUIDANCE*
*CHAKRA CLEARING*

*Oracle Cards*  (44 divination cards and guidebook)
*GODDESS GUIDANCE ORACLE CARDS*
*HEALING WITH THE ANGELS ORACLE CARDS*
*HEALING WITH THE FAIRIES ORACLE CARDS*
*MESSAGES FROM YOUR ANGELS ORACLE CARDS*
(card pack and booklet)
*MAGICAL MERMAIDS AND DOLPHINS ORACLE CARDS*
ARCHANGEL ORACLE CARDS

ॐ  ॐ  ॐ

All of the above are available at your local bookstore, or may
be ordered by visiting: Hay House USA: **www.hayhouse.com®**;
Hay House Australia: **www.hayhouse.com.au;** Hay House UK:
**www.hayhouse.co.uk;** Hay House South Africa:
**www.hayhouse.co.za;** Hay House India:
**www.hayhouse.co.in**

Dr. Virtue's Website: **www.AngelTherapy.com**

ॐ  ॐ  ॐ

# HEALING *with the* ANGELS

## How the Angels Can Assist You in Every Area of Your Life

c‰ c‰ c‰

### DOREEN VIRTUE, Ph.D.

**HAY HOUSE, INC.**
Carlsbad, California • New York City
London • Sydney • Johannesburg
Vancouver • Hong Kong • New Delhi

**Published and distributed in the United States by:** Hay House, Inc.: www.hay house.com • **Published and distributed in Australia by:** Hay House Australia Pty. Ltd.: www.hayhouse.com.au • **Published and distributed in the United Kingdom by:** Hay House UK, Ltd.: www.hayhouse.co.uk • **Published and distributed in the Republic of South Africa by:** Hay House SA (Pty), Ltd.: www.hayhouse.co.za • **Distributed in Canada by:** Raincoast: www.raincoast.com • **Published in India by:** Hay House Publishers India: www.hayhouse.co.in

*Editorial:* Jill Kramer • *Design:* Jenny Richards

**Library of Congress Cataloging-in-Publication Data**

Virtue, Doreen.
     Healing with the angels : how the angels can assist you in every area of your life /
Doreen Virtue.
        p.     cm.
     ISBN 1-56170-640-X  (trade paper)
     1. Angels—Miscellanea.  2. Guides (Spiritualism)  3. Spiritual healing—Miscellanea.  I. Title.
     BF1623.A53V57  1999
     2291.2'15—dc21                  99-42778
                                            CIP

ISBN 13: 978-1-56170-640-2
ISBN 10: 1-56170-640-X

13 12 11 10    40 39 38 37
1st printing, October 1999
37th printing, March 2010

Printed in the United States of America

To those who serve as angels,
in heaven and upon the earth.
Thank you for your love, dedication, and service.
Please continue to have patience with us
while we learn how to accept
your gifts with gratitude and grace.

# Contents

# Acknowledgments

Thank you to God, Holy Spirit, Jesus, Frederique, Pearl, and my other guides and angels. Much love and gratitude to Louise L. Hay, Reid Tracy, Jill Kramer, Christy Salinas, Jeannie Liberati, Jenny Richards, Margarete Nielsen, Jacqui Clark, Kristina Tracy, Karen Johnson, Ron Tillinghast, Joe Coburn, Anna Almanza, Suzy Mikhail, Adrian Sandoval, and Lisa Kelm.

I very much appreciate the angelic help I've received from Steve Prutting, Charles Schenk, Bronny Daniels, Janine Cooper, and Jennifer Chipperfield. Thank you to all the wonderful men and women to whom I have given angel readings, and angel blessings to my clients and students who allowed me to print their case studies and stories in this book.

# Introduction

It's not your imagination. Angels *are* among us, now more than ever, and not just in commercial venues. Increasing numbers of people are reporting encounters with these heavenly beings. In their encounters, angels deliver timely messages, healing remedies, and lifesaving measures.

Why are angels circling our globe so much lately? Partly because of our prayers for heavenly assistance, and partly because God and the angels know that it's time for us to heal ourselves, our lives, and our world. As we move through the millennium shift, the angels are helping us heal the challenges and ills that keep us from living at our highest potential.

The angels are here to teach us that God's love answers all questions and challenges. They are here to heal us from the effects of fear. The angels are powerful healers, and you can work with them to speed up their healing efforts. The more we invite angels into our lives, the more readily our lives reflect the splendor of heaven.

There are no limits to angels' healing power. They can help us heal our relationships, career concerns, finances, housing issues, and any other challenge that is troubling us. We just need to follow a few steps to help the angels help us:

1. **Ask**—The Law of Free Will says that angels cannot intervene in our lives without our express permission. The only exception is if we are in a life-threatening situ-

ation, before it is our time to go. Otherwise, we must ask the angels to help us.

How do you ask? you may wonder. No formal invocation is necessary to invite angels to help you. You simply need to think, *Angels!* and they will instantly respond. You, like everyone else, already have two or more guardian angels with you from birth until death. Nothing you can ever do, say, or think could make your angels leave you or love you less. Their love for you is powerful and unconditional!

You can also ask for more angels to join you. Either ask God to send angels to you, or call upon the angels directly. Both ways are identical, because the angels always answer to God's will. And God always wills angels to surround and comfort you whenever you ask.

2. **Surrender the problem**—Before God and the angels can heal your situation, you must completely give it up to them. It's a little like mailing a letter: You must release the letter from your hand before the post office can deliver it for you. So often we ask heaven to help us. Yet instead of letting this happen, we hold on to the situation, thereby blocking the angels' ability to intervene. If you really want help, completely release the problem to God and the angels!

3. **Trust in God**—We mustn't give God and the angels a script, in which we outline what steps we want them to follow to resolve our situation. Instead, trust that God's infinite wisdom and creativity will come up with a much better solution than our human minds could ever dream of. Remember: God's will is that you be happy!

4. **Follow God's directions**—After you release the problem to God and the angels, they may ask you to take
some human steps to resolve the situation. These directives will come to you as either a voice, a dream, a vision,
a knowingness, or an intuitive feeling.

If you're unsure of the source of these messages, ask
God for validation. God and the angels will always give
you loving and supportive messages, so if you ever
receive a fearful or hurtful directive, do not follow it!
However, if we stick closely to God in our hearts and
minds, we needn't worry about so-called fallen angels
interfering with us. God's Divine love is the only power
that exists. The thought-forms of fear and darkness are
illusions that can only "harm" us if we give them power.
Therefore, after you've asked the angels for help, watch
for God-given messages that will direct you on how to
resolve your challenging situations. These directives are
the answers to your prayers, and you must take action to
help God to help you. Sometimes these directions will be
action based, and the angels will ask you to go to a certain place or call a specific person, for example.

Other times, the directives will involve your mind
and heart, such as when the angels ask you to forgive
yourself or another. Whatever their messages, know that
they come from the Source of all healing and solutions.
By following these directions, your situation will be
completely healed.

No situation is too big or too small for the angels to
resolve it for you. Whether you want a parking space,
money for your bills, or better health, the angels are
happy to oblige. Their greatest reward is your happiness,
so if it fits with God's will, they will give you whatever
brings you joy. After all, joy is your birthright, and you
deserve it!

## Healing Someone Else

What if you wish the angels to conduct a healing on another person? For example, you'd like the angels to help a loved one in need, or a group of people in the news who have touched your heart.

It's always an act of love to ask God to send angels to another person's side. This is not a violation of the other person's free will, since they can choose whether to listen to the angels' messages. So, it is a good idea to ask the angels to surround others. God especially responds quickly to this request when it comes from parents who wish to have angelic "babysitters" attend to their children.

The angels will never usurp God's will, so if it is your loved one's "time," the angels will bring that person comfort and joy during their final days on Earth. A wonderful prayer for you to hold in your heart is, "Thy will be done." In that way, you can save yourself needless worry, and rest assured that God is taking care of everything perfectly.

## Archangel Raphael: The Supreme Healer Among Angels

For physical challenges such as illness or pain, there is no better healer among the angelic realm than the archangel Raphael. This angel, whose name means "God Heals," can bring instant release from suffering. Raphael glows with a beautiful emerald green healing energy. Often, the archangel surrounds painful body parts with this healing light. The light acts as a soothing balm, and as a trigger for sudden and complete healings.

Raphael, like all the inhabitants of the spirit world, can be with everyone who calls upon him simultaneously. Limitations of time or space do not restrict him. So, never fear that you are interfering with Raphael's other duties when you call on him.

The healing archangel comes to your side the instant you ask for him. You can call him by thinking or saying aloud, "Raphael, please help me!" Raphael will also join the side of your loved ones, at your request.

Raphael is a powerful healer who acts like a spiritual surgeon in releasing fear and darkness from our body and mind. Sometimes, however, we call upon Raphael and then we get in the way of his healing function. For instance, we don't allow him access to our "guilty secrets" so that he can extract them from us. Or, we try to help him along by telling him what to do. Although well intended, our human actions clumsily get in the archangel's way. Consequently, after you call upon Raphael, it's best to give him full access to your body, mind, and heart. In this way, he can fulfill his God-given function to heal everything completely.

No matter if it's a hangnail or a seemingly terminal illness, call upon God and the angels for help. They don't want us to wait until we're desperate or terrified before we do so. As the angels wrote through me in the book, *Angel Therapy*:

> Call upon God's heavenly creations for help and assis-
> tance as soon as you become aware of your inner pain. A wise
> homeowner who smells smoke does not wait until the home is
> engulfed by flames before telephoning the fire department. At
> that point, such a call feels almost useless. Do not wait until
> you are overwhelmed by monumental fear before calling upon
> God's name.
>
> At that moment—as in all times—He will send help and
> comfort to your side. Even so, you may not feel His loving arms
> for several minutes, as you feel barriered between many layers
> of fear and heaven. Smarter still is one who learns to monitor
> his own well-being, and who hesitates not in calling upon a
> heavenly creation of any form for assistance and comfort.
>
> Learn this lesson well, then, sweetest child, and remember
> always to care for your inner being by calling forth help when-
> ever needed. In that way, your ebb and flow of fear has not

sharp divides, but gentle swellings that do not erode your peace of mind.

The angels are here to help you heal your life, and they want you to ask for help.

# CHAPTER ONE

# Blessings and Challenges of the Spiritual Path

What drew you to study spirituality? A desire to explore the *truths* of life? A search for happiness, fulfillment, and inner love? A tragedy or miraculous happenstance that pushed you to explore the spiritual side of existence? Or were you intrigued by someone's example; perhaps a spiritually minded person whom you admire?

Whatever attracted you to this path, the common thread was your desire to improve your life. Whether you sought enlightenment, answers, new skills, or peace of mind, you believed that spirituality had something positive to offer you.

## *Happiness Is Holy*

Some of my clients were raised in religions that promote suffering as a virtue. These belief systems applaud martyr lifestyles;

and they create breeding grounds for guilt, fear, and resentment. So, when these individuals hop on to a spiritual path that promises happiness and abundance, they get nervous. *Are happiness and abundance "correct" goals?* they secretly wonder.

Those raised in Christian ideologies learn Jesus' teaching that it's easier for a camel to pass through the eye of a needle than for a rich man to enter the kingdom of heaven. Yet, in other passages, Jesus emphasizes that we should knock, and doors will open. Repeatedly, he urges us to have faith that our material needs will be met.

Most spiritual seekers understand that Jesus didn't mean to say that money was evil. Instead, he meant that the *obsession* with money was a deterrent to happiness in this life and the afterlife. Yet, obsession with money is a two-way street: Those who chronically worry about whether they'll have enough funds to pay their bills are spiritually identical to those who obsessively hoard their dollars. Both types of money obsession are rooted in the fear of not having enough. And this underlying fear robs us of happiness.

When we believe that suffering and lack are normal, or if we believe they are tests from God, we accept pain as a part of life. However, when we believe that God is 100 percent abundant love, and that God's creations are in His image and likeness, it follows that He didn't create pain or limitations.

In my long discussions with God, the angels, and Jesus, I'm convinced that God doesn't want us to suffer in any way. God, like any loving parent, wills for us to have happy, peaceful, and safe lives. God wants us to focus our time and energy on helping others, using our natural talents and interests. While we help others, He'll take care of supplying us with enough time, money, intelligence, creativity, and anything else we need. God knows that if we worry about having enough, we'll waste time and energy that could be put to better use.

So, God and the angels truly *want* to help us! However, because of the law of free will, they are only allowed to help us if we ask. This is a book that will help you know the rich experiences available to those who *do* ask.

### Angels and the Millennium Shift

You are very fortunate to be alive at this time in human history. For that matter, any time we are alive, it is a miracle. The angels have taught me that more souls want an Earth life than there are bodies to accommodate them. Souls actually stand in line, awaiting Divine assignments on Earth. The fact that you are here, in a human body, signifies that you are a winner. God chose you to come here, knowing that you have many gifts and talents that will benefit His other children.

The angels write this to you:

*"You, like everyone else who is incarnated at this time, are a holy and perfect child of God. We realize you may not always feel perfect and holy, and we also realize that you often don't act that way. Nonetheless, God created your soul as a literal 'chip off the old block.' It contains God-essence, or Divine light, that can never be extinguished, soiled, or taken away from you. Nothing you could ever do would eradicate your Divine heritage."*

The reason why this is a good time to be alive is because we are nearing the end of an era in which humans behave like aggressive animals devoid of spiritual awareness. We are at the edge of a time when we will collectively recover our spiritual gifts of intuition and healing. When intuition becomes accepted as a normal human characteristic, watch out, because the world is going to change drastically!

Think, for a moment, about a world populated by highly accurate intuitives. The more we accept this skill as innate, the more we will open our channels of Divine and psychic communication. Scientific studies conducted at leading universities such as Princeton, the University of Nevada, the University of Ohio, and Cornell already show evidence that each of us is potentially gifted in sending and receiving telepathic information. I say "potentially," because like any gift, we have to be aware of and practice it before we can truly master its usage.

Many people are becoming intuitive and opening themselves to Divine guidance. In my private practice, I'm awestruck by the number of high-level professionals—both male and female—who ask me for angel readings. These are folks who may have never thought about life after death, God, or spiritual issues three or four years ago. But now, in this spiritual renaissance in which we all find ourselves, the collective consciousness is looking heavenward.

Think for a moment about what our world will look like when we all regain our natural intuitive awareness. No one will be able to lie to another person ("little white lies" will fade into distant memories), which will definitely create shifts in our legal, educational, and political systems. Also, we won't need technological devices to communicate with each other.

I believe that a number of us have a life purpose that involves teaching others about their true spiritual origins. Many people, I believe, are still asleep with respect to the knowledge of their inner Divinity! They see themselves as a body, floating like a hapless cork, dependent on the current to tell it what to do. God and the angels know differently, however. They are aware that we create our reality through our conscious decisions and intentions.

*"Your intentions create your experiences"* is one of the angels' favorite phrases. What they mean is that our expectations, deep down in our heart and mind, are the scriptwriters of the movie we experience and call "life." If you ask yourself before entering any situation, "What do I truly expect to occur here?"

you will become the world's greatest psychic. That's because your expectations will literally predict what will happen to you.

### The Refining Process

Our tastes shift as a result of our spiritual study. We lose the desire for mood-altering substances, we're repelled by violence in the media, and our attraction to friends and lovers changes. The angels explain a lot of these changes as being a result of our "frequency shifting." They say that each person has a vibrational frequency that is visible to them, much like when we view a car's system on an oscilloscope or a person's brainwaves over a monitoring machine.

The angels say that our frequency adjusts according to our thoughts and emotions. Those who worry, fret, and obsess have slow frequencies, while those who meditate and pray regularly have higher frequencies. As our frequencies shift upward, we become attracted to higher-vibrating situations, people, food, and energies. This also means that we won't be attracted to some of the friends and events that once captivated us.

Vibrations surrounding ego issues, such as anger, violence, a lack mentality (believing there isn't enough to go around), a victim mentality (believing that other people control you or are to blame for your unhappiness), competitiveness, dishonesty, and jealousy are extremely low. High vibrations surround spiritual-mindedness, such as meditation, prayer, devotion, selfless service, volunteerism, healing work, teaching, sharing, and expressions of love.

The angels suggest that we avoid lower-vibrating situations as a means of pulling up our spiritual frequencies. They are particularly adamant about avoiding reports in the print and broadcast media that promote negativity.

Here are transcripts from two of my angel therapy sessions, in which the angels asked my clients to avoid this type of media:

**Doreen:** There's a message coming in from your angels. They're saying that when you read, watch, or listen to the news, it is upsetting to you and is negatively shifting your energy in a way that is counter to what you want. This is a very strong cautionary message to you. The angels say, *"Don't take this casually."*

**Barbara:** That makes sense. I listen to the news a lot on the radio, and it does upset me, so I guess I'll reduce how much I listen to it.

During another session, the angels explained how my client's low self-esteem was exacerbated by the negative images and messages she received from watching soap operas and other dramas:

**Michelle:** At times I feel like a total let-down or failure, not just to myself, but to my husband and daughter. Have I done something wrong, or what am I not doing? I love my family very much and would do anything for them, but when it comes to my husband, things have changed (I think). Something is missing, and how do I—or we—get that back?

**Doreen:** You have done nothing wrong, although the angels show me that there is the influence of the media around you, affecting your thoughts and therefore affecting your life. Are you watching a lot of TV? [Michelle confirms that she is].

It looks like you are absorbing negativity from TV shows, and this is influencing your thoughts and life. Can you try shutting off the TV for a week and see if that makes a difference?

Michelle took her angels' advice and found that within one week, she no longer ran "worst-case scenario" films in her mind. She dropped the habit of viewing her life through a negative soap opera lens, and she was able to see the gentle beauty in her family life.

### Shifting Your Frequency

The angels are here to help us heal in many ways, from issues and challenges that are seemingly mundane, to those that seem urgent or spiritually profound. One of the angels' healing tasks is to help us shift our vibrational frequency to its highest and finest rate. They want us to make this shift for two reasons. One is that this is a process of "ascension." We are all on the pathway of discovering that we are one with God. When we truly understand and live this knowledge, we are in the state of ascension.

That sort of knowledge profoundly affects your every interaction with others. Think for a moment how your life would be if you were consciously aware that everyone with whom you talked was a Divine aspect of your God-self. You would feel complete and total love for these individuals and for yourself. You would experience life as a heaven-on-earth experience.

The second reason why the angels want us to increase our frequency is because we will be better suited to our changing material world. The millennium shift is going to bring about significant positive changes in our educational, government, legal, and telecommunications systems. Our eating habits will drastically change, and our life expectancy will significantly increase.

The higher our frequency, the easier it will be to adapt to these shifts. We will be intuitively aware of pending Earth changes, in the way animals can foresee earthquakes and storms. Our high-frequency bodies will be able to teletransport, dematerialize, and withstand events that would traumatize a denser, lower-frequency body. Higher-vibrating minds will be able to manifest any required foods or other supplies.

So, the angels want to help you adapt to a changing world by giving you energy and guidance that will shift your frequency. The angels help you do so by giving you signs and signals, Divine guidance, and by intervening into your life and body. In this way, they help you maintain peace of mind. After all, peacefulness is one of our primary goals in life, and the angels are here to help us attain that end. Our angels sing with joy when they see us feeling peaceful and happy. In the next chapter, we'll look at how the angels play a part in our romantic relationships.

# CHAPTER TWO

# Angelic Interventions in Your Love Life

The angels can help us heal our relationship problems if we ask for their help. Mentally call to your guardian angel, or to the angel of the other person in the relationship, and witness the miracles that occur.

### Finding New Love

A woman named Beth asked her angels to help her find "Mr. Right," and they went to work immediately as heavenly matchmakers. She told me the following story about how the angels helped her heal her love life:

> I never really thought much about angels, but one day I heard you mention on a radio show that you have to ask the angels for help. So, I decided to give it a try. I asked them if

they could help find a good man for me. Less than a week later, I met a wonderful man. We clicked instantly. I believe he and I were meant for each other. The goals and things we have in common are awesome. So, needless to say, I have a new outlook on angels. I've started asking for their help more often.

## The Couple That Forgives Together . . .

The angels also help couples in committed relationships strengthen their bonds of love. Barbara was a student in my spiritual counseling course. She excelled at angel readings and had wonderful studying and homework skills. Barbara truly was interested in, and committed to learning about, spirituality and healing. During one of the classes, I conducted angel readings on a few of the students. Barbara was one of them.

Her question to the angels, during our session, concerned the fact that she and her husband, John, had been arguing a lot. She asked whether the angels saw a divorce coming, or whether she was supposed to stay in the marriage. Through me, the angels said, *"The purpose of your marriage is complete. You now have the option of staying together or parting ways. It is completely your choice."* Barbara decided she wanted to stay married, so she began praying for spiritual intervention.

I'll let Barbara describe what happened after she surrendered her marriage to God and the angels:

My husband and I had been dealing with marital problems for about a year. Sunday evening after the angel-reading session in which I gave my marriage to God, my husband hit a spiritual bottom. For many months, we both had been living in resentment and bitterness toward each other. After going into a rage, John asked me if we could talk. I knew the angels were protecting me because I had asked them to surround me, and I was very calm through all of this.

John told me he didn't know where God was in our turbulent marriage. I reminded him that God can't work through us unless we let Him in. Well, at that moment, John did cry out for God to come in and help him. The angels were also nudging me, saying, *"Okay, Barbara, you know what to do! It's time to start walking your talk!"* I walked him through the Forgiveness Corral Exercise [this powerful healing exercise is reproduced in the Appendix of this book].

I explained to John about the ego, and told him that it was our egos who were arguing—not our true selves. We shared into the wee hours of the morning about God and our spiritual beliefs. Our relationship turned a major corner. I stayed home from work with John the next day, and we continued to share and rebuild. It was an incredible experience. We talked about us both making the choice to recommit ourselves to our love and to our relationship.

The next day, on a beautiful sunny Saturday, John and I completed the "Forgiveness, Free Yourself Now" exercise [this exercise, required for graduating from my spiritual counseling certification program, also appears in this book's Appendix]. We drove to one of our favorite spots and found a place where there was a stream with a very small waterfall, so we could hear water flowing.

We sat side-by-side, but in parallel worlds, each working silently on our own forgiveness list. When I finished my list, I walked down to the water to do the releasement part of the exercise. The two names at the end of the list were John's and mine. I forgave myself down by the water, but saved the releasement of forgiveness with John to do in person once I rejoined him on the embankment.

Before leaving the stream, I saw a tiny lavender butterfly flutter beside me. John told me that as he said each person's name on his forgiveness list, he mentally held the person in his hand, then opened his hand and released the person as a butterfly. After we completely forgave and released each other, we continued to enjoy the beauty and serenity of our surroundings.

We both felt so light and free!

The love we currently feel toward one another and toward ourselves is unlike anything we have felt! It is as if both of us have been through, as John put it, a spiritual, emotional, mental, and physical overhaul! There has been such positive movement this week.

I am convinced that John's unforgiveness toward himself was what was at the root of his depression. Now that the unforgiveness is gone, the veil of depression is lifting. My own resentment and bitterness toward him are dissolved as well. Our forgiveness of ourselves and each other has allowed us to see one another through new eyes. It amazes me how diminished we had both allowed our internal sparks to become, and how that spark has once again become a flame.

## Probable Futures

The angels rarely say that our future is set in stone. Instead, they say our probable futures are based on our current train of thought. If my clients' thought patterns shift in a significantly positive or negative way, so will their future. This is what they explained to my client, Kevin, when he expressed fears about his future and marriage:

**Kevin:** My child will be leaving home shortly—mostly, I believe, to get away from the way things are here. I can't say I blame him. Things are not always pleasant; in fact, sometimes they get pretty bad. After he leaves, will he be okay, and what will become of my home life? Will it get better or worse? Will my spouse and I remain together or go our separate ways?

**Doreen:** The angels say that you are going through some major changes right now. They are grateful that you are contemplating your inner world and are taking responsibility for many parts of your life. The angels caution you, however, not to blame yourself; just to take inventory and make adjustments to your course based on your assessment.

Your marriage isn't set in stone right now. You truly have the power to save the marriage and make it work; however, you must have faith and keep a loving, positive outlook. You may need to get additional support to keep this positive outlook, such as a counselor, a spiritual study group, or a close friend to talk to.

No one is blaming you for anything, except in your expectations. However, if you believe that others are blaming you, you will experience this as a self-fulfilling prophecy. We certainly hope that you will make the choice to experience the miracles of healing that the angels seek to help you enjoy. You will be in my prayers.

## Love Never Dies

The following case shows how a good marriage is truly forever, even when one spouse dies. Often, the deceased spouse becomes an angelic matchmaker for the survivor:

**Annette:** I have been seeing a guy whose wife passed away, and I feel that someone is telling me it's okay. Could this be a message from an angel or even his wife? I feel it's a comforting message.

**Doreen:** Yes, you are very intuitive! His wife is encouraging you in this relationship because she can see the positive effect it has on him. She is above any feelings of jealousy and just wants to see love—the only thing that is real and that matters—to shine radiantly in both of you.

Congratulations on manifesting a wonderful relationship
and for being in touch with your natural gifts of intuition!

## Ma Bell, Angel Bell

The angels always emphasize the importance of truthful and
clear communications in our relationships. A therapist who has
taken my angel therapy courses reported the following case of
how the angels helped a couple to clearly communicate:

> My client had tried numerous times to get her boyfriend
> on her cell phone but kept getting only static. She was really
> upset because she needed to get in touch with him right away.
> I then suggested (knowing one of her guardian angel's names
> was Bell), "Why not ask Bell to help you?" She did, and the
> very next moment, the line was perfectly clear, and she was
> able to deliver her urgent message! Afterward, she said she
> never thought to ask her angels for something like that.

## Angel Prayers for Your Love Life

Here are two examples of prayers to use while working with
the angels to heal your love life. Make your own variations of
these prayers to suit your circumstances if you'd like. You can say
prayers aloud, mentally or in written form. God and the angels
hear all your thoughts, feelings, and intentions. Prayer is a very
powerful way to connect with heaven for the purposes of healing.

### PRAYER TO FIND A SOULMATE

*Dear God,*

*I ask that You and the romance angels help me be in a wonderful love relationship with my soulmate. Please give me clear guidance to find my soulmate, and help us to meet and enjoy one another without delay. I ask for Your help in creating circumstances so that I may be in this wonderful soulmate relationship right away. Please help me heal and release any blocks in my mind, body, or emotions that would make me afraid of great love. Please help me hear and follow Your Divine guidance that leads me to find and enjoy this soulmate relationship. I know that my soulmate is searching for me with the same amount of fervor with which I am searching for this person. We both ask that You bring us together and help us know and accept the blessings of great love. Thank You.*

### PRAYER TO HEAL AN EXISTING LOVE RELATIONSHIP

*Dearest God,*

*I ask that You and the angels help me heal my love life. I am willing to release any unforgiveness I may be harboring toward myself and my partner, and I ask that the angels cleanse me of all anger or resentment now. Please help my partner and me see each other through the eyes of love. I ask that all effects of our mistakes be undone in all directions of time. Please work with my partner so that we may have harmony, romance, friendship, respect, honesty, and great love for one another. Please renew our love. Thank You.*

Love is already within each of us, and we don't need another person in our lives in order to feel loved. However, the expression of love from and to another person is deeply satisfying. That is why the angels are so interested in helping us attain and maintain a soulmate relationship. They also want to help us in other types of relationships, such as friendships and with our family members, as you'll read in the following chapter.

# CHAPTER THREE

# Angel Blessings for Your Family

J ust as the angels help us in our love relationships, they also heal our interactions with our children and other family members.

### The Angels and the New Children of Light

There is a new "breed" of humans among us, according to the angels. They are highly psychic, strong-willed, extremely imaginative, and they are here to usher in the new age of peace. These powerful and intuitive people have little tolerance for dishonesty, and they don't know how to cope with pointless discussions or meaningless tasks. After all, their souls elected to incarnate on Earth at this time so that they could teach others about the importance of speaking truthfully and living in harmony.

Who are these mystery people? They are frequently referred to as "Children of the Light," "Millennium Children," and "Indigo Children." They are individuals who were born in the 1980s and '90s so that they could reach adulthood by 2012, the predicted time of the new age of peace. An entire book, to which I am a contributing author, is available through Hay House on this topic. It is called *Indigo Children,* by Lee Carroll and Jan Tober.

The trouble is, these special children are growing up at the tail end of the old energy in which people still lie to each other, still compete because of a belief in limited resources, and still engage in meaningless activities. Without coping skills to deal with these residues of our soon-to-be-former civilization, these children feel raw and vulnerable.

For example, let's say that Bobby is a nine-year-old Child of the Light. As a youngster, he saw angels and communicated clearly with them. He often sees visions of the future, and he makes psychic predictions to friends and family members that prove accurate. Bobby is outspoken, and he doesn't mind sharing his opinion when he feels an injustice has occurred.

At school, Bobby has difficulty coping with what he perceives to be meaningless activities. He knows, deep in his soul, that the current educational system will be replaced with one more applicable to everyday living. Yet, he is living in the age of the *current* educational system, and he must find a way to cope. Fortunately, many of Bobby's peers feel exactly the same way, since they, too, are Children of the Light. So at least Bobby doesn't feel all alone.

Bobby intuitively knows that he has a great purpose to accomplish in this lifetime. He senses that he is going to help many people, yet he's not quite sure how that will happen. All he knows is that whenever he wakes up, he feels as if his soul has traveled to a faraway school where he's taught subjects that truly interest him and that seem highly meaningful—things such as the geometric basis of matter, the universal laws of cause and effect, and studies on the probable future of Earth and humankind.

In contrast, learning about Christopher Columbus and grammar seems inconsequential to him. He feels bored and restless, and his attention wanders. Finally, his teacher sends Bobby to the school psychologist, who refers him to a medical doctor for evaluation. The diagnosis is quick and swift: attention deficit disorder (ADD). His mother fills Bobby's Ritalin prescription on the way home.

Bobby *does* feel better while taking Ritalin. Things don't quite seem to matter to him as much when he's taking it. The drug makes Bobby feel less irritated by the fact that his homework assignments are irrelevant to his life's purpose. In fact, Ritalin makes Bobby not care about a lot of things—such as talking to angels and engaging in soul travel at night. Thanks to his diagnosis and prescription, Bobby is now just a normal person who can't remember his mission in life.

### It's All about Integrity

The angels say that the years preceding and immediately following the millennium are devoted to helping us learn about integrity. In other words, our collective current life mission is to be true to ourselves. It also means being true to others, and that includes our children.

A decade or so ago, we psychologists warned parents not to confuse friendship with parenting. We lectured parents against having heart-to-heart discussions with their children lest they "parentify" their youngsters (meaning giving the children information that they were too young to handle).

Yet, the new millennium children require emotional and conversational intimacy with others. They thrive on honesty! If a Child of the Light feels that something is wrong, for example, in her parent's marriage, it's destructive for the parents to cover up this fact. It's so much healthier for parents to openly discuss (using terms and phrases that are age-appropriate to the child) the situation, than to have the child believe she is crazy for having feelings that run counter to what her parents are saying.

The angels have very strong opinions about these children, partly because the angels feel protective of them. Angels guard Children of the Light to ensure that their mission is completed. They say:

> *"Listen well, parents of the '90s. You, too, have an exceedingly important mission to fulfill. You must ensure that your children remain intuitive and that they stay very close to nature. Don't push them to succeed at the expense of losing their soul purpose, for our purpose is our guiding force, and without direction, your children will feel lost, alone, and afraid.*
>
> *"So much better for you parents to focus your children's attention on spiritual studies, as this is their true nourishment that will ensure their growth and survival. We angels are here to help you parent, and we won't interfere or get in the way. Simply allow us to cast a new light on difficult situations, a task we complete with joy in our hearts, simply by your open invitation for us to heal. Do not ever feel that God doesn't hear your prayers, for He sends us to your side the instant you call."*

In the cases that follow, you'll see how the angels have strong and sure guidance for parents. They discuss every seeming aspect of child-rearing, from conception to dealing with adolescent behavior challenges. I believe that the angels are extra-concerned with our children. In a way, after all, our children are God's Earth angels who are here for an important mission.

### Storks and Angels

My own parents had a miraculous experience surrounding my conception, which is part of the reason why they immersed me in spiritual studies while I was growing up. Childless after several years of marriage, my parents desperately wanted to have a baby. Finally, my mother put in a prayer request to a New Thought church, asking that the parishioners pray for her to conceive. She became pregnant with me three weeks later.

Many of my clients and audience members ask questions about conception and childbirth. I'm frequently asked, "When will we have a child?" "What sex will my newborn baby be?" and "Will my unborn child be born healthy?" As you'll read, the angels handle these questions with forthrightness and love.

Very often, I talk with the spirits of children who stay with their mother following a miscarriage or abortion. The children are happy and well adjusted and simply want to be with their mother to help and guide her. Or, if their mother gets pregnant again, they may have "first dibs" on inhabiting the new body and be born as a healthy baby. Those who don't have the opportunity to be reborn grow up on the other side, at about the same rate they would have if they had come to full-term births. Aborted children hold no grudges, by the way. Their souls are as intact as ever.

### Angel Nannies

The angels remind me of loving nursemaids and nannies. Like Mary Poppins, the angels take a firm but kind stance when it comes to how we raise our children (who are really God's children, in their eyes). The angels are blunt and direct but always loving. They love to be called upon for child-rearing questions and assistance!

**Janet:** I have two beautiful daughters, and I am pregnant with another child. I want to know if the angels can tell me how can I be a better mother spiritually to my children?

I was very sensitive as a child and talked to people on the ceiling until my own fears sent them away. My brother, who died when I was eight, came to me in my dreams. My oldest daughter is scared of the dark, talks in her sleep, and has nightmares that she never remembers in the morning. Is she afraid of spirits, angels, or some past-life memories? How can I encourage her to not be fearful? I think it is because she knows that there are always spirits and angels around, and maybe she can't see them but senses or hears them.

When I was her age, I was afraid of the voices I heard and blocked them out, and now I want them to come back because I am ready for them. My youngest daughter is just a light. She is happy, and I have a terrible fear periodically that she will be taken away from me. Can you please tell me how I can be a better mother to them?

**Doreen:** The angels say that you are a *wonderful* mom! They remind you that your intentions are the most important thing, and that you have very sincere intentions to be a great mom. That is all that counts—your sincere intentions!

Your children are definitely seeing and interacting with angels, and yes, that can be frightening for them at times. Just holding them, talking to them, and being there for them, plus always telling them your true feelings, is what is needed from you right now.

You are feeling a little drained and emotional because of your pregnancy, and this is making you feel a bit guilty. You feel as if you can't be everything to everyone right now, and it's true! This is a period of adjustment for all of you, a time to allow your children to grow up a bit so that you aren't always drained. This will help you feel more energized and cheerful, which is actually the gift your children most want from you.

## Angels and Adolescent Issues

God and the angels are brilliant helpers when it comes to the challenges presented by our adolescent children. All we have to do is ask and then follow their awesome advice, as my counseling student Jackie Saunders did:

> *Jackie's teenage son had been having terrible problems at home and at school, and Jackie was so upset that she had become physically ill. In desperation, she turned to God for help. "I need a miracle, God," Jackie firmly said. "I need You to help me help my son right away."*
>
> *A few minutes later, Jackie heard a distinct voice tell her,* "Go to Danny's Family Car Wash right now." *Jackie knew that Divine guidance sometimes comes in bizarre ways, but this seemed way over the top. "Danny's Family Car Wash?" she questioned. Then, in confirmation of what she had heard, the voice said,* "Yes, go to Danny's Family Car Wash right now . . . and hurry!"
>
> *So Jackie hurried into her car, not quite sure why, but obediently following the voice's dictates. As soon as she pulled into the car wash, the attendant told her, "We are going to wax and detail your car for half price." Jackie argued that she didn't have enough time. The attendant said, "Yes, you do." So Jackie surrendered to the situation and allowed her car to be detailed.*
>
> *As she sat waiting for her car, Jackie noticed a slumbering man in the corner with a pile of books lying on his*

belly. On closer look, Jackie saw that they were books on "adolescent psychology." Without thinking, Jackie woke the man up and asked him about his interest in teenage behavior.

The man shook himself awake and smiled as he explained how his own teenage son had once been a source of trouble. Then he discovered a psychologist who worked miracles with adolescent boys. Now his son was doing very well. These were books that the psychologist had recommended that the man read.

Jackie shook with excitement. "Please, please let me have the name of the psychologist!" she implored. As the man gave Jackie the psychologist's name and number, she felt that her prayer for help had been heard and answered. She drove home feeling peaceful, and planned to call the psychologist in the next couple of days to make an appointment for her son.

The next morning, Jackie woke up close to six A.M. She heard the inner voice that had counseled her to drive to the car wash. This time it said, "Call the doctor right now," referring to the adolescent psychologist.

"But it's only six in the morning!" Jackie argued.

"Call the doctor right now," the voice repeated. "She is leaving town very soon, and you need to call her now."

Trusting the guidance, Jackie called the psychologist and apologized for calling so early. Jackie could tell that she'd woken the doctor up, and feared alienating her. Then Jackie explained the reason for her call, "Please, I need to make an appointment for my son to see you."

"But I'm leaving to go out of town this afternoon," the doctor said. "Besides, I only work with five teenagers at a time, and I already have six in my case load."

Jackie knew that her Divine guidance wouldn't have led her to this doctor without reason, so she per-

*sisted. "I can't explain it," Jackie said, "but I know that it's very important that my son see you right away."*

*Something in Jackie's voice must have impressed the doctor, or perhaps the angels intervened. Regardless, Jackie breathed a sigh of relief when the doctor said, "Okay, I'll see your son this morning at 8:30. It's the only time I have before I leave for my one-week trip."*

*The doctor ended up taking Jackie's son as a client, and he thrived under the psychologist's care. Today, Jackie's son is happy and well adjusted, and she is grateful that God and the angels led her to Danny's Family Car Wash as an answer to her prayers!*

### Angelic Healings

More than 300 well-documented studies show that prayer has a statistically significant effect on healing our physical bodies. Researchers know that a placebo effect and wishful thinking don't explain this phenomenon. After all, many of the studies involve subjects who don't know they are being prayed for. This includes studies in which prayers showed positive effects on plants and infant babies, who may feel, but don't consciously know, when they are being prayed for.

Many of the prayer studies are "double-blind," meaning that the researchers and physicians—as well as the patients—don't know if they're being prayed for or not. Nevertheless, those who are prayed for generally live longer, heal faster, and require fewer medications than those who aren't prayed for.

I've received dozens of unsolicited testimonials from those who say that they, or their family members, have been healed because they prayed to have healing angels sent to them. In the following case study, my counseling student Karen Montano reported that her daughter Jourdan even saw the angel involved with her healing!

I'll let Karen tell you her story first-hand:

> My husband and I had to take our daughter Jourdan (age 6) to the hospital emergency room. She was running a fever of 104 and suffering from back and abdominal pain. Before the doctor came into the treatment room, I closed my eyes in prayer, calling Archangel Michael and all my daughter's angels to be in the room.
>
> When I opened my eyes, I saw a family friend who had passed away last year standing at the foot of the gurney toward her head! He seemed to be conducting some sort of hands-on healing work over her.
>
> I then saw my aunt, whom I loved dearly and who just passed over six weeks ago, at the doorway. She smiled at me and said, "Everything will be all right!" and then she turned her head. Then, as if she were directing traffic, I saw her waving her arms to the souls that were wandering in the hallway telling them, "Everything is all right! There is no need for you to be in this room. It's okay . . . just keep on going . . . keep on moving toward the light!" It was the most peaceful experience, and I knew everything was going to be fine.
>
> Jourdan is home now, feeling fine. She says she clearly remembers my aunt working on her body and helping her to heal.

## A Child's Eternal Love

Some of my most heart-wrenching sessions involve talking to my clients' deceased children. I've conducted several sessions where children who died via suicide explained their reasons and delivered profuse apologies. I've talked to dozens of adolescents who died in tragic car accidents. And, I've helped parents of murdered children understand the sequence of events surrounding their child's death.

Often, these cases bring tears to my eyes. Here is a session that was particularly poignant, in which a deceased young man sends his love to his living mother.

**Ginny:** Do you see anything about my son who died?

**Doreen:** What is his name?

**Ginny:** Robert.

**Doreen:** Okay, Robert, Robert. [I say a person's name repeatedly to call them from the afterlife plane. After about two minutes of calling Robert, I saw a tall young man appear next to Ginny's side.] Was he tall?

**Ginny:** Yes.

**Doreen:** I'm seeing a tall young man step next to you right now. He's very gangly, with a youthful face. He also dresses kind of old-fashioned. His face is so youthful that it's tough to know how old he was. He could have been anywhere in the 18 to 25 bracket.

**Ginny:** Yes, that's him. He was 22 and mentally handicapped.

**Doreen:** He's next to your left side, although he's not always with you. Robert is very quiet and has a serene energy. He makes a motion that he's having a lot of fun on the other side. He's showing me an image of himself running. I don't know if you know much about the afterlife plane, but there are many different levels and layers. In some of the afterlife areas, it looks just like the most beautiful parts of Earth.

People in the afterlife plane create these images of Earthlike life from their mental images. Robert lives in a very rural type of area, and he's showing me himself running through a wheat field with his arms outstretched as if he's flying.

**Ginny:** He loved the farm.

**Doreen:** Well, he lives in a farmlike area in the afterlife plane, and he says that he feels very free. He says, "Mommy, don't be sad." He prints out a letter *J*, or is it *I*? Did Robert know how to write?

**Ginny:** He could write his name and a few simple words.

**Doreen:** Oh, okay, it is an *I*, and he's writing out, "I love you."

ॐ ॐ ॐ

### *Changing Relationships and the Spiritual Path*

Obviously, the study of spirituality can change your life in many different ways. It opens you to new possibilities, miraculous interventions, and healings. It also shifts your relationships considerably.

The issue of relationships is probably the greatest concern of those on the spiritual path. You may worry, "Will my friends and family still relate to me, with my newfound interests and different perspectives on life?" You may find yourself losing interest in old friends and craving new friendships with like-minded people.

You might also be concerned with how your family will react to your spiritual path. Those raised in traditional religions may receive flack from family members who view metaphysics and nontraditional spirituality through fearful eyes.

Changes are inevitable when you open your mind, heart, and life to Spirit. These changes can be wondrous, beautiful experiences if you allow yourself to trust the process. They can also be frightening and painful if you grip tightly to attachments of how you think things *should* be, or if you fear losing people. Such fears often prove self-fulfilling.

Fortunately, the angels are available to guide you through these changes and to smooth the way.

### Changing Mind-Sets, Changing Friendships

"Through my spiritual studies, I made some decisions to change how I lived," an audience member named Celia explained to me. "First, I decided to stop gossiping and talking down about people. My spiritual studies made me aware that I was actually hurting myself every time I gossiped or put down someone else."

Celia was initially uncomfortable with this decision because she and her best friends regularly engaged in gossip as a group pastime. How would her friends react if she didn't join in? So, Celia asked for Divine guidance about how to handle the situation. What she received, through intuitive emotional feelings, was a true answer to her prayers.

"I knew that I was to help my friends learn that it's more fun *not* to gossip than it is *to* gossip!" Celia explained. "After all, we only did this because we thought it was the best way to have fun. So, I leveled with my friends one night and said, 'Look, this type of talk is really holding us all back. Let's stop it, and make a pact to say something if we ever hear one of us start to gossip.'

"So, whenever anyone in our group starts to talk negatively about someone or something, someone else in the group will speak up and say, 'Oops!' or something like that to call attention to the gossip. What we found is that gossip was a habit we'd all gotten into, and it took us some time to break that habit. All of us feel so much better now that we're sharing more positive things when we talk."

As Celia pointed out, when we go through behavioral transitions as a result of our spiritual path, it's an opportunity for us to be a way-shower or teacher to our friends and family. This is a tricky balancing act, however. Nobody—especially our friends and family—wants to receive sermons or lectures. The best way to teach peace is to demonstrate it through our actions. If we scream at our friends or family, "Why can't you be as spiritual as I am?" they pay attention to our demeanor and discount our words.

Ask the angels to guide your actions and words so that you can be a truly effective teacher to others.

### Chakras and the Law of Attraction

True Divine guidance never speaks in terms of blame, guilt, or whether someone is right, wrong, good, or bad. So, your angels always seek out a win-win resolution to conflict. However, they may occasionally guide you away from relationships and help you close the door on a friendship whose purpose has been served.

Ending a relationship can feel frightening to anyone, but for those on the spiritual path, this process can elicit extra guilt. "I'm supposed to help people and be a loving person," you may worry. "Am I abandoning my friend if I choose to spend less time with her?"

The truth is that you may choose to spend less time with old friends, and more time with new people in your life. This does not mean that you are judging, criticizing, or abandoning anyone. You are not being a snob or isolating yourself. You are simply allowing yourself to be guided according to the spiritual law of attraction.

We are attracted to people whose mind-sets mirror our own. It's a matter of common interests creating friendships. As your lifestyle shifts, you will naturally look for people with whom you have things in common. On an even deeper and metaphysical level, your mind-set affects the energy centers in your body, which are called "chakras." Each chakra corresponds to a different life issue. Whatever issue we spend the most time thinking about determines which of our chakras are stimulated. Then, as if by radar, we attract and are attracted to people with similar mind-sets.

The angels explain that the chakras send out energy waves that bounce back like a sonar system. When we meet someone with a similar energy pattern, their chakra energy bounces back to us in a feel-good way. We are then attracted to them and are pleasantly surprised to find that we share mutual interests.

For instance, if you think about money and security most of the time, your first chakra will be affected. This is called the "root chakra," which is located at the base of the spine. Like a magnet, you will pull other people into your friendship circle who also have money and security concerns.

The second chakra, called the "sacral chakra," is concerned with body issues. This chakra is located midway between your navel and tailbone. People with physical challenges or obsessions surrounding weight, physical appetites, health, or addictions will have out-of-balance sacral chakras. You will tend to attract and be attracted to other people with body issues.

Issues that affect the third chakra, or "solar plexus," include fears or obsessions about power and control. This chakra is housed in our midsection, behind our navel. If these issues are on our mind a lot, we draw people to us with similar mind-sets.

The three lower chakras are concerned with Earthly matters. The fourth, or "heart chakra," is the first of a set of chakras concerned with higher issues. Not coincidentally, the spiritually centered chakras are located higher up in the body. The heart chakra, located in the chest, concerns itself with love. Those who are working on love issues, such as forgiveness, compassion, and soulmate relationships, are called "heart-centered." They tend to attract other loving people into their lives.

The fifth chakra, located in the Adam's apple area and called the "throat chakra," is concerned with creative expression and communication. Those involved with artistic or teaching projects—particularly of a spiritual nature—invoke the energy of their throat chakra. This chakra is especially stimulated by an integrity lifestyle, where you strive to always have your words and actions match your inner truth. By concentrating on these issues, you pull like-minded souls to you.

"The third eye" is the sixth chakra, which centers around spiritual sight and visions. If you have been visualizing and meditating, or if you are naturally clairvoyant, this chakra is opened. You will draw people of similar spiritual interests and abilities into your life.

"The ear chakras," located just above the eyebrows on the left and right side, deal with listening to Spirit. Those who silently meditate and tune in to the messages of heaven have stimulated their ear chakras and tend to attract other listeners.

On the inside of the top of the head is the "crown chakra," which is activated when a person realizes we are all one with God and each other. A person with this mind-set will naturally attract like-minded souls who share the spiritual path.

So, let's say that in the past, most of your thoughts were centered around Earthly matters such as money worries or sexual obsessions. Your circle of friends shared similar beliefs. Then you had a spiritual awakening that led you to read and meditate about Divine topics. In doing so, your primary chakra energy moved upward. So, instead of operating out of your first (money-related) or second (sex-related) chakra, you began living from the fourth (love-related) or fifth (truth-related) chakra.

As soon as this shift occurred, you would naturally lose the "pull" you once felt for people who live from your former chakra mind-set. You will either begin to desire, or start to attract, people who share your focus. Through the law of attraction—as long as you hold a positive expectation—new, like-minded friends will enter your life.

## CHAKRA CHART

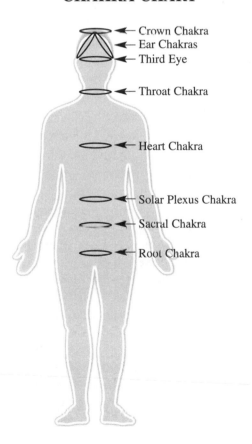

◄— Crown Chakra
◄— Ear Chakras
◄— Third Eye

◄— Throat Chakra

◄— Heart Chakra

◄— Solar Plexus Chakra

◄— Sacral Chakra

◄— Root Chakra

### The Law of Attraction and Running into Friends

A man named Charles related this story of synchronicity:

> I was Christmas shopping in a mall near Boston when my friend and I walked into a department store at the exact moment as a young woman who had attended college with us several years before. I was just talking about her earlier that morning, saying that I hadn't seen her in years and wouldn't it be nice if I could see her again soon?

Events such as the one above are validation that this is a Divinely ordered universe. Instead of worrying about how things will work out, we need to put our time and energy into holding positive thoughts about what we desire. Through the law of attraction, we will draw those situations and experiences into our lives.

Maria Stephenson, a spiritual counselor from Arizona, said that the following experience helped her know that she and her friends were being watched over—not only by the law of attraction, but by helpful angels as well.

> A group of us from Phoenix were meeting at a hotel in Newport Beach for a conference. Several of us were sharing rooms to cut down on the expenses. Late on Friday, I arrived at the hotel and assumed that everyone in our group had already checked in, since the others were scheduled to arrive several hours before me. I checked to see if they were registered, and they weren't. So, I registered and went to the room to wait for the others to arrive. Time went by, and somewhere around 8:30, I fell asleep waiting.
>
> At about 10:40, I heard a voice in my sleep telling me to *"wake up."* I sat up and looked around. No one was there. I laid my head back on the pillow and wondered where my friends were. I again had a strong feeling, and a voice in my head said,

*"Get up, get on your shoes, and go out the door."* I attempted to dismiss it again, but the feeling got stronger. So, I got up, put on my shoes, and went to the door. As soon as I opened the door, there were my friends walking down the hall!

The hotel had made a mistake and had failed to put the room in my name, instead, putting it in a completely different name. So here were my friends, getting another room and having to pay for it separately since they could not find me! They were literally about to put the key in the door! If I had not walked out right then, they would have gone into their new room, and I would have never seen them. We would have been paying for two rooms. We all could not believe what had just happened. Not only had I just caught them, but the chance of them being on the exact same floor. . . . Of course, then we laughed and knew exactly what happened—thanks to my persistent angels waking me up and getting me out the door!

### Angelic Healings for Family Members

A woman named Cheryl Anne shares this story of how the angels healed her sister and her dog:

I woke up early one morning to pray for my sister who was going through horrible trials in her personal life. Even her dog was sick. I prayed for her, then blew the flame of my prayer candle out. It would not go out. I repeatedly tried to extinguish it, then realized what was happening.

I closed my eyes and sat quietly there in the candle's glow. Then they came to me, the guardian angels of my niece, nephew, and sister—and yes, even the dog! They were so clear and announced their names and purposes. My sister had two angels, one on each side of her, one male, one female. Their names were Michael Edward and Ruth Ann.

I wrote an e-mail to my sister to tell her what I had been shown. She was not a person of faith, so I was concerned that she would laugh at me or be angry, and yet I knew I had to tell her. She gasped as I told her their names. She told me of a dream she had the night before: She was being pursued by a man and a woman. She ran from them, but they kept calling to her, saying, "Don't run. You need us!" When she began to wake up, she heard herself calling out what she thought was a name or strange word. She decided to write it down so she'd remember. The word she was yelling in her sleep, the word she had written down at her bedside, was "MERA."

She asked me to repeat the angels' names. When I told her, "Michael Edward, Ruth Ann," which MERA stands for, I'm not sure who was more startled! Most of my previous encounters have been very personal, and other people haven't received any sort of signs relating to them. It's always just been me and my weirdness! (By the way, her dog, who was close to death and was surrounded by tiny birdlike angelic creatures that morning, is doing just fine!)

My sister is now doing very well. She had considered herself an atheist for many years and is now in the midst of a spiritual awakening. Her dear little dog is completely healed as well. It has been an amazing time for her family. Although they have dealt with tremendous difficulty this past year, their lives are now being flooded with love and light from God and their guardian angels.

### Prayers to Heal Family Relationships

Here are some examples of powerful prayers that you can say (either mentally, aloud, or in writing) to ask God and the angels to intervene in your family life. Please add or rewrite the messages in the prayers to fit your specific circumstances.

## PRAYER TO CONCEIVE A BABY

*Dear God,*

*We have so much love to give, and my spouse and I want to share our love with a baby. We ask that You and the angels help us conceive. Please send one of your brightest and happiest souls into our life, and let this being become our baby child. Thank You.*

## PRAYER TO HEAL PARENT-CHILD RELATIONSHIPS

*Dearest God,*

*Please help my child and me have a harmonious relationship. I ask Your help in healing any fears that interfere with my child and me expressing love to one another. Please help my child to focus and feel happy. Please help my child accept me and my circumstances. I ask that You and the angels help my child and me release our unforgiveness and resentment. Please help us have a loving and close relationship. Amen.*

## PRAYER FOR CHILDHOOD BEHAVIORAL ISSUES

*Dear God,*

*Please help me understand my child. I ask that You surround my child with love, wisdom, and intelligence. Please help my child understand and accept responsibility for his/her behavior. I ask that You guide my child to make intelligent choices based upon love, not fear. I ask that You and Archangel Michael please clear my child of any attachments or blocks that could be interfering with his/her happiness. Thank You.*

### PRAYER TO HEAL FAMILY RELATIONSHIPS

*Dear God,*

*I know that my family member and I both have guardian angels. I ask that these guardian angels help us heal our issues and misunderstandings. Please help us release any anger or unforgiveness. I ask that all effects of our mistakes be lifted and forgotten by everyone involved. Please help me release any judgment I may be carrying toward myself or others. I ask that our guardian angels clearly give us Your direction, knowing that Your will for us is peace. Thank You.*

### PRAYER FOR A FAMILY MEMBER

*Dearest God,*

*Please help my family member feel peace and happiness at this time. I ask that You send my family member extra angels to comfort him/her. Please surround our entire family with an extra cushion of Your Divine love. Help us to relax and to have faith and trust. Please give us a sign of Your love so that we may release our fears. Thank You for all of Your healing love.*

### PRAYER FOR A FRIENDSHIP THAT IS ENDING

*Beloved Creator,*

*I know, deep down, that my friendship with _____ is ending. I ask Your help to accept this transition with grace and peace. I ask that You and the angels help me be honest in a loving way, with myself, and with my friend. Please help me be true to myself so that my actions stem from love instead of from fear, guilt, or obli-*

*gation. Please comfort my friend so that we can both accept this change in a positive way.*

## Prayer to Attract New Friends

*Dearest God,*

*I now see myself surrounded by loving friends with whom I share much in common. I can feel the presence of new friendships with like-minded souls, and I ask Your help in manifesting this vision. Please guide me to meet new people who are positive, spiritually minded, health conscious, and fun. Please help me to know that I deserve the love and attention of these new friends. Thank You so much.*

# CHAPTER FOUR

# *Your Ascending Body*

The angels help us heal from physical challenges. They also want to help us have more energy and vitality, so they offer us guidance on how to take good care of our physical selves. As with all aspects of working with angels, we must ask the angels to help us before they are allowed to intervene. The only exception is a life-endangering situation that occurs before it's "our time" to go.

### The Angels and Sleep

During an angel reading session, the angels taught me that it's important for us to have a good night's sleep so that they can better help us. This is a transcript of a session (related to sleep issues) between myself and a first-time client I'll call Rhonda. Please keep in mind when reading this that this is my first session with Rhonda, and I don't know anything about her.

I purposely only write people's names down when they make an appointment with me to avoid being influenced by advance information. Also, I work with the angels in three ways: Either I'll relay what I hear them say in my right ear, like a translator; or I'll describe the clairvoyant images that the angels show me; or the angels speak directly *through* me, indicated by the use of pronouns such as *we* or *our*.

> **Doreen**: Your angels say they are working with you in your sleep. *On* your sleep and *in* your sleep, they say. There's a message that you need deeper sleep. [The angels show me a light coming into her bedroom and waking her up.]. Is there some sort of interruption coming during your sleep from a light?

> **Rhonda**: Yes, I work the graveyard shift right now, and I sleep during daytime hours, and the sunlight comes into my bedroom while I'm trying to sleep.

> **Doreen**: Oh, okay, that's what the angels mean. Can you close the curtains more, or the blinds?

> **Rhonda**: I've got the blinds closed, but they still let sunlight peak through. I've got to put something additional up on the windows.

> **Doreen**: Most definitely, because your angels say that this light wakes you up, and they say it's not letting you go into a deep enough sleep. Without the deep sleep, the angels can't go into your dream state and interact with you. They're very concerned about your sleep.

> **Rhonda**: Okay, I have these other curtains to put up over the other blinds, but I've been procrastinating putting them up.

**Doreen**: Yes, your angels *really, really* want you to have deeper sleep, and they say to block out that light.

**Rhonda** [later in the session]: My mind has been chattering a lot lately. Is there any type of meditation, sound, or mantra I could do that would help quiet my mind?

**Doreen**: The angels say, *"We feel that the main thing you could do to help your mind is to get a better night's sleep by blocking out that light. You'll see the inner light if you block out the outer light! You don't need any other tools but to have a good night's sleep. We angels are seeking to work with you. We knock on your door each night, but you have to be in a deep level of sleep for us to access you. You're not reaching that deep level, and it's affecting your concentration."*

ॐ ॐ ॐ

Not only do the angels give advice about the importance of sound sleeping, but they also help us sleep well. All we need to do is ask them for assistance. A friend of my husband's named Terry explained his positive experience in working with the angels in this regard: "I had been working really hard and was due to have another difficult time the following day. I was feeling exhausted and needed to have a solid night's sleep. So I asked my angels to help me. It worked! I had an excellent night's sleep and awoke refreshed."

### Soul Traveling and Dreams

During this angel reading session, my client Katherine and I discussed the phenomenon of having out-of-body experiences during sleep. Very often, our angels escort us to other-worldly places where we attend school and learn deep spiritual lessons. Other times, we may actually be involved in teaching others during these experiences of soul traveling.

**Doreen:** I see that you do a lot of soul traveling in your sleep and that you sort of remember these travels as dreams, but you don't quite remember the dreams in the morning.

**Katherine:** I ask my angels to help me remember my dreams, but I still can't remember them!

**Doreen:** When you do soul traveling, you go into a fourth-dimensional world where things are not based on time or space. Those are beliefs of this third-dimensional world, beliefs that limit our ability to understand basics of life. So, you are learning about truths that don't translate, or don't make sense, when you wake up with a third-dimensional mind-set. However, all of your dreamtime learning and experiences are incorporated into your unconscious and *do* influence you in a positive way. So it's not necessary to remember these soul travels and dreamtime lessons in order to benefit from them.

### *Angel Energy*

Now you know that the angels will help us sleep well if we ask for, and follow, their guidance. By doing so, we awaken refreshed and energized. There's no reason for us to feel tired, as the angels say that we have an unlimited source of energy in and around us. That source is omnipresent God, who is within you right now.

If you feel tired for no apparent reason, mentally ask the Archangel Michael to come to you by saying a prayer such as this one:

### PRAYER FOR INCREASED ENERGY

*Archangel Michael, I ask you and your helpers to come to me now. Please cut away and release anything that is draining me. Help to lift my energy to its natural state of vitality now. Thank you.*

ॐ ॐ ॐ

You will feel the presence of this mighty angel soon after saying such a prayer. Using his "sword," Michael removes attachments that are draining you, as well as the negative energy that is weighing you down. Within minutes, you feel refreshed and revitalized. I find that this method works ten times better than drinking coffee.

A woman named Pam also discovered that the angels could help her stay awake during a long, late-night drive:

> One day, my friend and I were driving home from Las Vegas. As he was driving, his eyes started to get heavy, almost closing. We were both tired, but he seemed to be worse off than I was. I took over driving, but after a while, my eyes started getting heavy and kept closing, too.
>
> Suddenly, out of nowhere, I got a burst of energy. Less than a minute later, a car went from the far right lane and darted across three lanes. The car missed the center divider as it then spun around and stopped blocking the lane we were traveling in. I was able to stop safely and just missed hitting the car by a matter of inches. Had this occurred only minutes earlier, I would have plowed into the other car while dozing off.

Needless to say, the adrenaline pumped through my body from the incident, and there was no longer a hint of drowsiness. We arrived home safely.

Prior to this incident, my friend had often spoken of angels, but I was not sure that I believed in them. I did not disbelieve; I was just skeptical with an open mind. This was the proof for me that there are guardian angels. While back on the road after the close call with the collision, I said, "Okay, I believe!" and thanked my angels for watching over me and my friend.

## Detoxifying Your Body

The angels urge us to detoxify our bodies, and you may have received some intuitive feelings that compel you to make changes in your diet and lifestyle. These are very real messages that you are receiving from your guardian angels. You are not imagining them.

The angels ask us to stop consuming toxins in the things we eat, drink, and use on our bodies. Toxins pull down our energy levels and make us feel sluggish. They also block our ability to clearly receive messages from heaven. Toxins also interfere with our spiritual growth.

The main toxins that the angels ask us to avoid are:

— *Meats, fowl, and fish, contaminated with hormones and pesticides.* Since virtually all animal flesh and by-products (milk, eggs, cheese, etc.) currently have residues of hormones and pesticides, you may consider adopting a vegetarian lifestyle or a near-vegetarian lifestyle (where you eliminate animal products once or twice a week). If you feel you must consume animal products, purchase "organic" dairy products (such as Horizon brand milk), and free-range chickens, hormone-free meat, and eggs from free-range chickens. These products are available at health food stores, as are wonderful meat and fowl substitutes, such as seitan, glutan, tempah, and baked tofu. Vegetarianism has come a long, long way in the past five years. If you haven't tried vegetarian meals in a while, give them another try—they're now delicious and difficult to distinguish from meat products.

— *Pesticides on fruits and vegetables.* Try to eat an all-organic diet. Ask your grocer to carry organic produce, or find a health food store or fruit stand in your area that sells organic fruits and vegetables.

— *Toxins in beverages.* The angels ask us to eliminate or significantly reduce alcohol, caffeine, and carbonation from our diet. Drink spring water, not "drinking water," as the angels urge us to drink water in as natural a form as possible. Drink fresh fruit juice, as the life force in fruits leaves 20 minutes after it is squeezed. Concentrated or refrigerated fruit juice has healthful vitamins, but it is not as life-giving as freshly squeezed juice.

— *Nitrates.* Avoid cured meats, such as lunch meats, sausage, and bacon. There are wonderful substitutes made from soy products that look, taste, and smell like the real thing. Many supermarkets carry these deli-substitute products, as do most health food stores.

— *Toxins in toiletry items.* Avoid laurel sodium sulphate, a nitrate catalyst, and Propylene Glycol, an industrial anti-freeze. Read the labels of your lotions, toothpastes, makeup, and shampoos. Weleda makes one of the only toothpastes that doesn't have laurel sodium sulphate as an ingredient (their "Plant Gel" and "Calendula" toothpastes are wonderful and can be ordered at 1-800-241-1030), and Aubrey makes great lotions (1-800-AUBREYH). Health food stores carry a wide variety of nontoxic products, but be sure to read the ingredient labels, because some so-called natural products have laurel sodium sulphate and other toxins in them.

— *Toxins in household products.* Avoid Cocamide DEA, DEA, Sodium Laurel Sulfate, Sodium Laureth Sulfate, Tallow, and Synthetic Fragrance. Health food stores carry natural and effective cleaners and detergents. Avoid bleach and bleached paper products, such as napkins and paper towels.

You can accelerate the detoxification process by drinking plenty of fluids and by getting adequate sleep, exercise, and fresh air. Drinking "wheat grass juice," which most juice bars and health food stores offer, can also pull metals and pollutants out of your body rapidly.

The angels say that they are working with us to increase the "vibrational frequency" of our bodies. Like a violin string that vibrates at a higher rate according to the note that is played, we are beginning to move up the scale ourselves. We are doing this to keep pace with Earth's accelerated vibrational frequency.

This doesn't mean that we move faster during the day, or that we become busier or more rushed. Vibrational frequency means that we are less dense and more sensitive to the higher, finer frequencies of the angelic realm. It means that we are more intuitive, creative, and naturally energized.

Many lightworkers feel guided to adopt a vegetarian diet. They then gradually get guidance to become a complete vegan (no animal products). After that, they are guided to eat only raw and unprocessed fruits, vegetables, nuts, and grains. Eventually, we are collectively moving toward a lifestyle of "breatharianism," where we'll receive all of our nourishment from the *prana* that is in the air. This will dramatically increase our life expectancies and ability to communicate telepathically.

If you feel compelled to delete certain foods or beverages from your diet, mentally ask your guardian angels to heal your cravings so that you won't miss the product. You'll be amazed at how easily you can give up toxic foods and drinks, if you'll ask the angels to assist you. Every week, I meet people who tell me that the angels eliminated or significantly reduced their cravings for alcohol, sugar, white bread, chocolate, colas, and other toxins. I had the same experience myself, where my cravings for junk food and coffee were completely removed.

Here's a wonderful prayer to say:

*Dear Angels,*

*Please surround me with your healing energy, and help me to heal my cravings for unhealthful foods and drinks. Please remove my desire for toxic substances, and help me to have the motivation to live and eat healthfully. Please guide me while shopping, preparing, and eating food, and give me guidance about how to live without polluting myself or my world. With great love and gratitude, I thank you.*

### Angel Healers, Angel Helpers

I also talk to many people who have been healed through prayer, conversations with God, and asking the angels for help. Fred Rothlisberger, a reader of my books, sent me the following story:

I was going to go in to have my third back surgery February 16, 1998. It had been several years since my last back surgery for a congenital problem. I was worried about being put out again, as I have a hard time coming out of anesthesia.

I was out in the back yard, cleaning up after our dogs, when a voice came to me. It simply stated, *"Don't worry about the surgery; it will be fine, God has more work for you to do."* I felt very peaceful from that point on. I had the surgery, and they found a cyst growing in my spine, which was putting pressure on the spinal cord, thus causing me my pain. I was released the day following the surgery to go home.

My recovery was very fast. I have had seven surgeries in my life, and never have I felt the peace and the speed of recovery I had with this surgery.

ॐ ॐ ॐ

A woman named Shelly Long "just happened" to turn on the radio the day I was on a local Phoenix, Arizona, station. Shelly was on her way to visit her doctor for a biopsy on a lump that had been discovered in her breast. She heard me emphasizing, "You must ask your angels to help you. Unless there's a life-endangering situation before your time, the angels can't intervene without your permission."

Shelly had always been a woman of faith, but she had forgotten to ask the angels to help her to heal. So she said a prayer, requesting the angels to intervene, and then pulled into the doctor's office. During the examination, the doctor was unable to find the lump. It had disappeared since her previous visit, one week earlier!

The angels love to assist us because they have complete faith, they retain a joyful attitude while helping us. The angels have taught me that a somber attitude often makes bad situations worse. Joy is the key to manifesting desired outcomes, including healing. In fact, the angels often display a wonderful sense of humor during their work with us, as Tina Needham's story illustrates:

> I've read a lot of books that have been profound and meaningful to me. But it wasn't until I read *Divine Guidance* that I felt I had an actual tool to help me reach a different and more "active" level. I was using Doreen's advice to clear blocks and meditate, when halfway through the book I had my first angelic experience. It was so "everyday" that it still makes me laugh. I didn't hear harps or see glowing visions.
>
> I was in bed next to my sleeping husband one night, wide

awake because of the cutting pain of a strep throat infection. I heard a woman's voice in my left ear. It said: *"Master, the throat lozenge is in the bottom drawer."* Definitely, not the profound message I was looking for!

I was numb. I laid there for a moment, trying to collect my thoughts, I even woke up my husband to see if he had said anything to me (even though it was a woman's voice). I tried to explain it away. I was a skeptic at heart, which is why I was trying to remove the blocks from seeing my angels in the first place.

You see I never, ever use throat lozenges, as I can't stand how they taste and feel. I sat up with my feet on the floor, took a deep breath, and pulled open the third and bottom drawer of my bedside table. It was dark, and I rummaged around the cluttered drawer until I felt it—old and sticky, but a Hall's Mentholatum lozenge. I got goose bumps all down my arm. I got up immediately and wrote the entire experience down. It was three A.M. I will never forget it. I still don't really understand the reference to "Master."

### Healing Effects of the Past

The angels aren't limited by time or space constrictions. Neither are we, but we don't sufficiently believe this yet, so we appear to be trapped in limited access to time and space.

If you have any regrets for past actions that are impacting your present-day health, the angels can help. For instance, if you abused your body with cigarettes, alcohol, or drugs in the past, your angels can help you undo the negative effects of these behaviors. The undoing will positively affect everyone involved, so, for example, any negative consequences that other people experienced because of your smoking (such as secondhand smoke) or intoxication will be healed.

Here is an angel prayer to help undo the effects of the past:

### Prayer to Undo the Effects of the Past

*Dearest Angels,*
*I have made mistakes in how I have treated my body,*
*and I ask that all effects of these mistakes be undone and*
*forgotten in all directions of time by everyone involved.*

## Life Expectancy

Part of the life plan that we develop before we incarnate is the length of time that we'll live. Together with our guides and angels, we decide if we'll live 40, 60, or 100 years. Most people opt to live long lives because they want to be with their children and other loved ones for a long time. However, other people decide to live shorter lives, either because they're reluctant to live on Earth for a century, or because they only have a brief lesson to learn before returning to heaven.

The new "Indigo Children" who were discussed earlier have higher life expectancies than previous generations. Many of these children will grow up in the new energy following the millennium shift and will live to extremely old ages. This will be because many of the conditions that are detrimental to health, such as ingesting a poor diet, bearing stress, and breathing in pollutants, won't be a factor. Humans will live in a fresh, clean world; we will consume a much more nutritious diet; and we won't compete or engage in other unhealthful activities.

The angels can tell you what your life expectancy is, if you'd like to know. When people find out their time frame for living, several positive results occur. I've watched certain individuals instantly heal from phobias after they learned that they were going to live many more years. Suddenly, they're able to release their fears of dying once they know that the end is not near. Of course, this isn't an invitation to "tempt fate" and begin jumping out of airplanes without a parachute. However, this knowledge can help people relax quite a bit.

Second, those who receive their life expectancy information become motivated to fulfill their goals now, instead of waiting for the future. They get going on the careers, hobbies, and ambitions because they know that they have a finite number of years in which to accomplish and enjoy them.

To find out your life expectancy, simply close your eyes and take a deep breath. Then, ask your guardian angels, "How old will I be when I leave the physical plane and return to the after-life plane? How old will I be in this lifetime when I pass on?"

You will either hear, see, feel, or know a set of numbers. Most people hear two or three numbers because you've selected these various ages as "outs." The first number you hear is an age when you could "go home" to heaven if you finish your mission and elect to leave. You can stay on and live to the second or third age if you like.

If you received an age that has already passed by, think for a moment about what happened to you at that age. Were you depressed, ill, suicidal, or in any accidents? If so, you chose to stay on Earth longer and live to the older ages that you originally chose.

If you are one of the souls who elected to be here for the millennium shift and beyond, you may find that you will live to an extremely old age, in the hundreds or even the thousands. As I wrote earlier, the life expectancy in the coming energy shift will dramatically increase.

You have free will, and I believe that you can elect to go home or stay here for longer or shorter periods than you originally designed. So if you don't like the life expectancy information you received, decide on a different number. In *A Course in Miracles*, it says that no one dies without their own consent. So, you are in charge, and your angels will help you fulfill these wishes.

## PRAYER FOR HEALTH AND HEALING

*Dear God,*

*I know that You created me in the perfect image and likeness of Yourself. I ask that You, Holy Spirit, and the archangel Raphael help me know and experience this health in my physical body. I am willing to release all thoughts and behaviors that create the illusion of illness and pain. I know that You are omnipresent, so therefore, You exist in every cell in my body. Please help me feel Your love in my physical body so that I can know that You cradle me in Your arms right now. Amen.*

## PRAYER FOR A LOVED ONE'S HEALTH

*Beloved God,*

*Thank You for sending the Archangel Raphael and the healing angels to my loved one's bedside. I now see that You, Holy Spirit, Raphael, and the angels are embracing my loved one. I picture my loved one smiling and feeling well. I know that, in truth, my loved one is well right now, and I ask for Your continued help so that we may realize this peace and health in our daily experience. Thy will be done.*

## PRAYER FOR WEIGHT AND APPETITE

*Dearest God,*

*Today, I have set my intention that my appetite for food be solely for healthful and light foods and beverages. I am willing to release any fears that would make me want to overeat. I know that You are guiding me in every moment of my life, including the times when I eat and drink. I ask that You continue to bless me with Divine wisdom and peace so that all of my decisions about consuming food and beverages will come from my higher self. Thank You, and amen.*

### PRAYER FOR SLEEP ISSUES

*To My Creator,*

*Please help me to have a restful and sound sleep tonight. I ask for a guardian angel to be posted on the north, south, east, and west sides of my home during the night. I visualize my home surrounded by the Divine white light of Your protective love. I am willing to release all of my cares and worries to You and the angels so that the pockets of my soul are emptied for the night. Please send some comforting angels to my side so that I may enjoy a wonderful night's sleep.*

### PRAYER FOR FITNESS MOTIVATION

*Dear God,*

*Please help me to be motivated to take good care of my body. I ask Your help in carrying through in my commitment to exercise, eat healthfully, and get sufficient rest. Please help me have faith in my ability to attain and maintain physical fitness. Please guide me to know the best ways to take care of myself. If my motivation slackens or I am tempted to procrastinate, please help me reaffirm my resolve. Thank You, and amen.*

### Prayer for Healing an Addiction

*Beloved God, Holy Spirit, and the Angels,*
*I know that addictive cravings are actually a craving*
*for Divine love. Please help me feel that I am filled with*
*Your ever-present love. I am willing to release any fears*
*that would block me from the awareness of Your love. I*
*ask you to clear away from me the beliefs, patterns, feel-*
*ings, and thoughts that trigger my cravings. Please guide*
*me to people, situations, and experiences that support my*
*desire to live free of addictions. I surrender all my crav-*
*ings to You, and ask for extra angels to surround me with*
*the light of health and peace. Please help me now and*
*always. Amen.*

So much of our health and life is affected by our careers, and the angels also want to help us heal our professional and financial lives. In the next chapter, you'll see how the angels guide us to remember our life's purpose and to find meaningful vocations and avocations.

# CHAPTER FIVE

# *Life Purpose and Your Career Path*

T he angels help us heal our career path, and they are very
empathetic to people who feel they are in the wrong job. The
angels see our hidden talents, and they know that we can help
others—while enjoying ourselves—by working in a profession
that incorporates our natural interests.

Many people come to me searching for their life purpose.
The angels are happy to help us remember the mission for which
we volunteered before incarnation. Sometimes their help comes
as psychological guidance, as in the case of my client Amy.

> **Amy**: Is there a message my angels want to give me about
> my life's path and direction?

> **Doreen**: I hear your angels say in unison, *"Be true to you!"*
> It seems that you are following your career path some-
> what, but you are still compromising the true desire of

your heart. They tell me that you rationalize your feelings about your career and that you are praying for help. The answer to your prayers has already been given to you, and you are aware of it: Be honest with yourself, and take steps based upon that self-honesty. God and the angels will guide you step by step in what to say and do, in a loving way, and be assured that they will never ask you to do anything that would bring harm to you or others.

## Finding Your Life Purpose

"What is my purpose?" is one of the most common questions that my clients pose. They ask this question because they desire meaningful work that makes a difference in the world. We each have a "Divine life purpose," which is an assignment we agreed to fulfill during our lifetime. God, our guides, and our angels helped us devise this purpose before our incarnation. They ensured that the purpose would mesh with our natural talents and interests. The plan also came with enough time, money, intelligence, creativity and other resources to fulfill it completely.

Annette was a retired widow who wanted to know about her life purpose and who felt a desire to contribute to the world. As the angels explained, we don't necessarily need to turn our life purpose into a paid vocation.

**Annette:** I wanted to find out about my life purpose because I want to do something that helps the world.

**Doreen:** Your angels say that you already are. They say, *"Not every purpose involves a nine-to-five job with a paycheck. Many purposes involve you merely being centered and peaceful when you're in town shopping. You are a messenger of Divine light and love. You are a role model to many, which* is a subtle, but important, purpose. *To be a role model, you don't necessarily have to be someone who is up on stage or in the newspapers. It can be someone, like yourself, who is a role model of peace, compassion, and gentleness."* They're showing me that these are your qualities and that other people do notice. The angels also show me that your gardening is a form of therapy for you.

**Annette:** Oh, I do like to garden!

**Doreen:** They give you the thumbs-up and say, *"Anytime you garden, you are contributing to the world through your peace of mind. Every time you have a peaceful thought, it goes out into the world and affects others, just as, conversely, angry thoughts affect others in the way that secondhand smoke does. When you are gardening, your thoughts play beautiful music that resonate throughout the spheres."* Your angels bless you for your contributions.

The angels say that you don't need to punch a time clock to make a contribution to the world. However, they also mention that if you *wanted* to do some volunteer work, you would be happy in an institutional setting such as a hospice. In your volunteer work, you would simply visit with the residents and put a hand on their shoulder and give them a kind word. Bring them tea. And while you're doing this, your loving and healing energy is going to them.

**Annette:** Yes, I *had* thought of doing hospice work!

**Doreen:** Well, that's one thing that the angels say you would enjoy and be very effective at, if you wanted to do some formal work outside the house. I see you going into the hospice residents' bedrooms and comforting them in a real simple, quiet, and loving way. Not so much what you say, but your countenance is healing to them.

**Annette**: That's my style, definitely.

**Doreen**: But your angels don't urge you to do this, Annette. Your angels say,"*This is a time in your life for you to slow down a bit, relax, and enjoy. Keep your pace under control.*"

**Annette**: Oh, that makes sense. I was so busy for so many years.

**Doreen**: They don't want you to push yourself or feel guilty. They want you to know that you are making a contribution to the world every time you have a peaceful thought.

ನ್ಲ ನ್ಲ ನ್ಲ

As Annette's angels explained, our main mission is to be at peace with ourselves. So our task involves "being" more than "doing." Yet, the desire to be of service to others is very strong in many people. There is a human fear of dying without having lived a life that has mattered. In the following session with my client Stella, we discuss how the drive to fulfill our purpose is practically instinctual:

**Stella**: I feel very compelled inside to achieve what I came here to do.

**Doreen**: Yes, of course.

**Stella**: And it's not the kind of feeling that just goes away over the years.

**Doreen**: No, nor can it. The urge that we each have to fulfill our purpose is an extremely strong instinct.

**Stella**: As I get older—I'm in my early '40s—I start to feel that I don't have that much time left. I've got to get started and do "it," whatever "it" is.

**Doreen**: Exactly. Purposes don't always have to be a paid profession. It's nice when that happens, but please don't discount how much you already help people when you talk to them, listen to them, and teach them. We'll talk with your angels during our session tonight and see what they say about your life's purpose. Deep down, you already know what your mission in life is. You've just forgotten it, and the angels will remind you if you ask for their help.

### Spiritually Meaningful Careers

Sometimes, my clients tell me that they long to help the world via a spiritually related profession. Many people are making significant contributions to the world in ways that seem quite subtle. For example, some people's life purpose is to "anchor light" to the world. This means that they are sent as radiant Earth angels who send healing thoughts and energy into Earth's body and atmosphere to undo the harmful effects of pollutants and negativity. In the following session, my client Belinda and I discuss the role that her upward vibrational frequency shift is having on the world:

> **Belinda**: Can you give me some idea about my mission in this life? I had thought for a long time that my mission was to be in a really great relationship, and from that, to raise our vibrational frequency as a couple. But lately, because I

can't find that type of a permanent relationship, I'm beginning to wonder if my mission involves something else.

**Doreen:** Yes, your mission does involve raising your vibrational frequency. By raising your frequency, you lift the whole world and provide a service. But you also learn the balance between humility and humbleness and really love yourself as you love your neighbor. You have some privacy and intimacy issues, and you're learning to balance this so you know how to deal with other people. You are also learning how to express yourself for therapeutic reasons.

You also have the path of the teacher, so art, writing, and creative expression are really important to your growth. I see newspapers all around you. When we began our session, I saw you writing, so this is an avenue for you to check out—journal writing, initially, and then see where it takes you.

**Belinda:** Well, I do love to write.

**Doreen:** The angels also show me that it would be a great idea for you to have pink roses around you.

**Belinda:** Oh, wow! That opens my heart just thinking about it!

**Doreen:** Exactly, pink roses are correlated with opening the heart chakra.

### The Artist's Soul

I find that people are happiest when they are in careers that match their true interests. Artistic people, such as my client

Eileen, need to be in creative careers. Some people think that they can't make much money in artistic ventures, but if we use our creative resources, we discover many practical and wonderful ways to make money artistically:

**Eileen:** At this age, I cannot afford to make many more career mistakes, and I ask that my angels guide me. Am I doing the right thing by marketing this computer product, or am I meant to do something else? I am tired and confused and do not want to get a real job.

**Doreen:** Your angels thank you for consulting them in this matter. They remind you that you are part of a team, and they love your team approach to your career. They also suggest that you come to them for other aspects of your life, including your relationships.

Your angels say that you have true artistic talents and not to let those go. You can have a job that you enjoy while you pursue your real passion simultaneously. Don't confuse the two and think that you have to suffer to make money until your real ship comes in. The computer marketing position, as you know, isn't suited to your real interests. You are just doing it for the money, and unfortunately, when we do that, we don't make as much money, *plus* we don't enjoy ourselves!

There is another job waiting for you. I see retail sales involving products for women at a boutique or some sort of store. It is low-stress, happy work, with upbeat customers. This will help your other career (it's something where you're self-employed in a creative venue) to zoom, because you'll feel happy and also financially secure.

**Eileen:** Thank you. I must ask who my angels are—and the other career, might it be catering?

**Doreen**: Catering would certainly fit the parameters of what your angels show me. Anything where you can use your artistic talents would work out very well! You have several angels around you, including Gabriel, the angel of artists and communicators. Other angels with you are Hoziel, Chamuel, and a male angel who insists that his name is Oscar.

## Boosting Your Business

One evening I gave a lecture to a group of healers from all different backgrounds on how the angels could help them in their private practices. During the talk, I mentioned that the healers could ask the angels to help them attract more clients. All they needed to do was say a prayer such as, "I ask that everyone who would receive blessings by being with me, be guided to come to my practice."

One of the counselors in the audience, named Elisabeth, experienced immediate success after she said this prayer. She wrote to me, "I attended your lecture in which you gave out the affirmations about how we can get more clients. I did so immediately and every day after. Right away, I received referrals, virtually overnight."

Another one of my spiritual counseling students named Nancine asked her angels to help her begin a public speaking career. Here is her story of how the angels Divinely guided her to give speeches:

> I am beginning a career in motivational speaking and have been meditating for quite some time about how to manifest an audience. By being still and quiet in meditation, I was able to hear my angels' Divine guidance. First, my angels encouraged me to look for the underlying block that surfaced if I imagined

really receiving my heart's desire, and to release this belief. When I did so, I realized I had an ego concern over whether I was really qualified and had enough credentials. So I wrote out the concern, among other beliefs, and burned them in a ceremony. I wrote out positive affirmations about my qualifications and placed them all around my house.

A few weeks later, I received a speaking request on my answer machine. When I was about to return the call, I heard a gentle voice within say, *"Go to the library first, sit in quiet, and make an outline before you call."* I followed that guidance and made an outline, then returned the call. The caller asked me if I could do a workshop on business marketing. With my new outline in front of me, I was able to confidently explain what I could do— right down to the workshop title! "Wonderful," the caller said. "Will three hours be sufficient, or would you like more time?" I suddenly had my first major speaking engagement, thanks to tuning in to my Divine guidance!

During the next eight weeks prior to my speaking engagement, I took time to clear my chakras and listen for Divine guidance. Each day, the angels would take me to the keyboard and begin to write. One day, they urged me to write a biography of my career background. The very next day, the speaking organization asked me to fax over my bio and the workshop outline. A week later, she mailed out hundreds of brochures with this information. I could not have waited a minute longer, which is what the angels had told me.

One of my guardian angels suggested that I contact a local news service and create some publicity. The new service's initial response was, "No interest." A few days later, the angels said, *"Let's call them again. Be loving, but be firm."* I thought this was crazy, but I did call, acknowledging their needs and expressing the good fit of my speech in their newspaper. On the morning of the seminar, one of my neighbors excitedly told me, "I saw your name and your event in the newspaper yesterday morning!" It was the only day I had not purchased a copy, but she gladly gave me hers. There it was, on the front page of the Business section.

When I gave the workshop, I was so pleased that my audience was filled with people of the highest energy. Truly, our experience together was perfect. The organization president wrote me later, "I could see from the beaming faces throughout the room that you had truly touched an inner core." The angels continue to guide me in my speaking career.

## Looking Our Best

The angels remind me of coaches, helping us to be our best at work. They prepare us in all way—intellectually, spiritually, mentally, and physically. For example, my husband, Michael, was getting ready to go to his office for the day. He knew that he wasn't going to be with clients during the morning and would be by himself at work until around noon, so he decided to skip shaving in the morning, and instead, packed his electric shaver so that he could shave in the mid-morning at the office. As he packed the shaver, he heard a voice say, *"Better pack the electric cord, too."* Michael thought this was odd, since his shaver is battery operated, and he had recently recharged the battery cell. Still, he listened to the voice and packed the cord. Three hours later, as Michael stood shaving at his office sink, the shaver's batteries suddenly died. "If I hadn't packed the electric cord, I would have been unshaven for my afternoon appointment," he said.

## A Pat on the Back

A woman named Patricia told me this enchanting story: "I had worked diligently on a very complex document. When I was finished, I silently said to my angels, 'This deserves some level of praise.' Upon delivering the document to my client, he called me later and indicated that he was totally impressed and actually thanked me for my creative efforts. This from a client who has never, ever given a compliment to anyone on staff. My angels and I rejoiced!"

### *Stress Management*

The angels continually tell me, *"All pressure is self-imposed."* In other words, stress is of our own choosing. We may con ourselves into thinking that someone or something else is making us do something against our will, but ultimately, we always have the choice and ability to say no, even if there are heavy consequences involved in doing so. The angels say that realizing we have this option is liberating and helps us to shed the stress that accompanies feeling like an imprisoned slave.

We have so much more control over our daily lives than we realize, often because we've never tested the waters to know how much our thoughts influence everything that comes to us during the day. The angels have taught me the importance of setting our intentions for the day, first thing in the morning. Decide, "What do I want today to be like?" and it will be done.

For instance, if you want the telephone to be quiet, ask your angels to screen your calls. People who normally would call you at the drop of a hat will be guided to not call you unless the news is really important. Conversely, if we expect the day to be a crazy zoo, that is the intention that will prove self-fulfilling.

My student, Bonnie, discovered this secret one day. A sales-person, Bonnie woke up one morning and said to her angels, "I really would like to work from home today." To her amazement, every phone call she received appeared to be Divinely guided. She recalls, "Everyone who phoned was requesting appointments for next week. That gave me the time I needed to take care of some long-overdue tasks. I am now taking charge of my day, instead of allowing circumstances to dictate my schedule. Now

I'm completing projects that I used to carry over each day and that used to weigh me down."

Your angels can function just like wonderfully loyal office managers and assistants. Ask them to manage your phone calls, visitors, and appointments. Invite your angels to brainstorm with you so that you can develop creative new ideas. They'll help you to make your meetings on time, and as I discovered, they won't let anything get in your way.

## Business Traveling

I'm on airplanes nearly every weekend, giving workshops in one or more cities. Flying this much would usually mean encountering a percentage of problems, but when you bring your angels along on trips, the statistics are more in your favor.

Because of the storms around the country, the Atlanta airport was practically shut down one Sunday night when I, and thousands of other travelers, were trying to catch planes. The only airline that was flying was Delta; all the other carriers cancelled their flights. So, everyone was pouring into the Delta terminal, struggling to get airline seats.

The Delta plane that I initially boarded for Los Angeles sat on the tarmac for 30 minutes. Then the pilot announced that because of mechanical problems, the flight was cancelled and we'd all have to leave and try to get seats on other flights.

We returned to the terminal amid a sea of people standing at a gate podium, demanding to be allowed on the only remaining flight in the airport going to California. Again, I prayed and asked the angels to help me get home. I was tired and had clients to see the next day. Somehow the crowd pushed me to the front of the line.

I began talking with a couple in front of me in line. We smiled and joked, while nervously noticing the many people who were mobbing the ticket counter. I felt that we were in the eye of a volatile hurricane. Then it was my new friends' turn to be next at the gate. The ticket agent said to them, "I've got three seats left on the plane. They're all in the rear, but they're yours if you want them."

The ticket agent looked at me, and then turned back to the couple and asked, "Is this person traveling with you, also?"

"Yes, she is," the couple replied. As I sank into my airplane seat moments later, which was miraculously an aisle seat, I thanked God, the angels, and the couple profusely for helping me.

### Angel Prayers

Here are some powerful prayers to help you connect with the Divine in your work life:

### PRAYER FOR HEALING JOB CONFLICTS

*Dear God,*

*My deepest desire is to be happy while I work, and I ask Your help so that I may find peace on the job. Please help me to be understood and understanding with everyone with whom I come into contact. Please clear me of any fears that trigger relationship conflicts in the workplace. I ask that You and the angels guide me to job responsibilities and tasks that match my interests and skills. I now visualize myself feeling happy when I wake up to go to work in the morning, and I ask Your assistance in manifesting this vision. Amen.*

### PRAYER FOR FINDING YOUR LIFE'S PURPOSE

*To Everyone Who Watches Over Me,*
  *I seem to have forgotten my Divine life purpose, and I ask your help so that I may remember the reason I chose to come here at this time. I am willing to release all fears that keep me from remembering my life's purpose, including the fear of success and failure. I know that I am qualified to fulfill my mission, and I ask for your continued guidance in helping me to know which path makes my heart sing. Please help me to know the difference between joy and fear so that I may immerse myself in meaningful actions that serve others and bring me joy. Thank you so much.*

### PRAYER FOR A NEW JOB

*Beloved Creator,*
  *You have guided me to find a new job, and I ask Your help in noticing the doors that You are opening for me now. I ask for very clear and evident signs to guide me to a new job in which my talents and interests are used in meaningful ways. Please help me to know that I deserve a wonderful new job, and allay any nervousness during the interview process. I ask for extra angels to boost my confidence and courage, and to keep me centered in the sure knowledge that You are providing for me now. Amen.*

## PRAYER FOR HEALING STRESS

*Dear God, Archangel Raphael,*
*and Archangel Michael,*

*It seems that stress is taking a toll on me, and I need your help. Please release me from the pressures that I have imposed upon myself. Raphael, I ask that you cover me with your healing energy so that my body will shed the effects of stress. Michael, I ask that you cut away the effects of negative and fearful thoughts, including cords that are draining me. I am willing to release any habits of self-punishment, time urgency, or other belief systems that create stressful situations. I know that I have sufficient time and energy, in truth, and I ask that you help me experience this sufficiency right now. Thank you, and amen.*

## PRAYER FOR INCREASED BUSINESS OPPORTUNITIES

*Dear God, Holy Spirit, Ascended*
*Masters, and the Angels,*

*I ask that everyone who would receive blessings from my business products and services be guided to contact me today. I welcome new people and opportunities into my life with open arms. I am willing to release any negative thoughts, patterns, or beliefs that would lead me to sabotage new opportunities. Please help me know that I deserve good now. Thank you.*

## PRAYER FOR FINANCIAL PEACE

*Dearest God,*

*I know that You are the source of all my good and that You provide for me in all ways. Please help me release the fears that block me from receiving Your gifts. Please help me feel the emotions of peace, gratitude, and financial security and to know that I am Your child upon whom You bestow great blessings. I now stay open to Divine guidance, which perfectly leads me to situations, people, and opportunities that are part of Your plan for my financial peace. I now see and feel myself and everyone else as completely financially secure, and my heart overflows with gratitude and joy at the abundant universe that You created. Thank You, and amen.*

### Angel Affirmations

I work with clients to increase their self-confidence, both by sending angels to release their self-doubts and by asking them to repeat "angel affirmations" on a daily basis. I've listed many of the angel affirmations that I use in my counseling practice in the Appendix of this book. You can use affirmations to heal issues related to your career, or to increase your self-confidence in social relationships, your love life, and in your relationship with yourself.

In working with people who feel frustrated in their jobs, or who have been unsuccessful in attaining their desired career, I usually find that a lack of self-confidence is the culprit. For instance, I had a client who was an actor. He hadn't landed a role in ten months at the time of our session. The angels told me that my client didn't expect to be hired, and that very negative expectation was affecting his performance. My client instantly realized the truth of this angel reading, and soon after, he worked with affirmations and his angels so that he would *expect* to be hired. He became a working actor again right away.

The angels want to become involved with every area of our work life. In the following chapter, you'll meet a special group of angels who can help boost your mood and energy levels.

# CHAPTER SIX

# *Nature and Animal Angels*

Did you ever notice how wonderful you feel when you walk outside? The nature angels, who live among plants and animals, are largely responsible for this therapeutic effect related to the great outdoors. One of the reasons why we feel wonderful when we're around plants, flowers, and animals is because nature is filled with powerful healing angels. Often referred to as "the elemental kingdom," nature angels are a realm of the angelic kingdom that can rapidly heal you of any challenge.

### Nature Angels—The Elementals

Every living creature has guardian angels, including flowers, plants, trees, birds, and animals. There are many different types of beings in the "elemental" or nature angel kingdom. These include creatures who are considered mythical, such as leprechauns, elves, tree people, and brownies.

When we open up to our clairvoyance, we find that these beings actually exist and that they aren't that difficult to see. All you need to do is walk in wilderness and mentally call out to them. It's important to have a polite attitude, as elementals are wary of humans who have aggressive, manipulative, drunken, or cocky outlooks. They love humans who are interested in ecological preservation, which is the primary purpose of the elemental kingdom.

The fairies are the elementals who are primarily involved in healing humans. They look like Tinkerbell, diminutive humanlike beings with dragonfly or butterfly wings. They flit from flower to flower, looking like fireflies with their whitish glow.

I meet many people who have fairies as guardian angels. These are always people who have a life purpose involving nature, ecology, or animals. In the chapter on incarnated angels, you'll read about humans who actually *originated* from the elemental kingdom.

The fairies help us release negative thoughts, thought-forms, and energies that we may have absorbed from others or from our own worries. When you walk in nature, mentally ask the fairies to surround you with their love and light. They will swarm around you and will pluck negativity from you like a bee collects pollen. The fairies also instill a sense of playfulness that will inspire you to laugh and have fun, which are certainly therapeutic activities.

You can find fairies wherever there are plants or animals. The greatest number of fairies are around flowers and areas of wilderness. Your potted houseplants have fairies with them, as well. This is one reason why having a potted plant next to your bedside is healthful: The fairies can work with you while you are sleeping and help you have a wonderful night's rest.

### *Animal Angels*

In many ways, our pets are our Earth angels. They provide us with companionship, unconditional love, and entertainment. What's wonderful is that each animal has guardian angels. So, when you are with your pet, you are not only interacting with your animal; you are also having close contact with your pet's guardian angels.

I was once asked by a talk show host if dogs' angels look like little dogs with wings. He then asked me if flies had angels (they do!). Animals have fairies as their guardian angels. Animals and birds who live in or upon water have "sylphs" as guardian angels. Sylphs are water fairies who are long, thin, and transparent, with an opalescent coloring. They do not have wings, as they swim instead of fly.

We can talk to our pets' guardian angels and ask for their help whenever there is a concern about our animal. Your pets' angels will help with challenges of all types, such as health challenges, behavioral problems, or in locating a lost animal.

Romeo, my cat, is a fluffy Himalayan with huge blue eyes and cream-colored fur. He has the strongest personality of any animal I have ever known, and everyone who meets him falls in love with him—hence, his name. In fact, if you put your face close to Romeo, he will put his tiny mouth close to yours as if he's kissing you.

Most of the time, Romeo is well behaved. Sure, he bosses my husband and me around by insisting that his plate be constantly overflowing with fresh food. Of course, it has to be the most expensive brand of cat food or he won't touch it. But beyond this idiosyncrasy, Romeo has never given us any trouble . . . except for that one day when he climbed onto the roof of our two-story home. Since the roof is made of tiles and sits at a steep angle, I feared that Romeo would slip and hurt himself. I know that cats are resilient in falls, yet I also worried that Romeo—a lifelong declawed housecat—might also run away from home in the panic of falling from the roof.

I ran to a window that adjoins the roof and pried off the screen, hoping to reach my beloved boy, but he stood about two feet from my outstretched arms. Too frightened to step out onto the slippery roof, I loudly pleaded with Romeo to come to me. He looked at me and blinked sleepily, but he made no motion to walk in my direction.

I looked at my watch. My husband and I were scheduled to leave the house for an important meeting. Yet, how could we leave the house with Romeo stranded on the roof? Finally, I realized I'd neglected to pray about the situation. Always, my past prayers had resulted in speedy action from the universe. But sometimes, in the midst of crises, I would "forget" to ask for spiritual help until I'd realize that my solo human efforts were ineffective.

It occurred to me to ask Romeo's guardian angels for help. Although I had never consciously thought about my cat having angels, at that moment, it seemed like a perfect solution. After all, doesn't everyone have guardian angels? Why would animals be excluded from this gift from God?

I closed my eyes and directed my prayers to my cat's guardian angels: "Please tell Romeo to come to me at the window and allow me to pick him up off of the roof." I felt a wave of peacefulness wash over me as I opened my eyes. I felt compelled to say, "Romeo, come here," and this time, it worked!

Romeo immediately walked over to me and allowed me to lift him into the house. My cat was safely in my arms as I shed tears of gratitude for the immediate help given by his guardian angels. All of us, including animals, are surrounded by guardian angels who provide love and protection.

### *Angelic Protection for Our Pets*

Renée, a woman who has taken several of my angel communication courses, also found that her own guardian angels provided protection for her pet cat. She related:

> I had a wonderful experience and want to share it. As always, before I go to sleep, I do as Doreen suggests, and ask God to place an angel on every corner of the house to protect us through the night. My son came home at two A.M. from work. He was tired and did not check to see if the house was locked up. He accidentally left the back door open—I mean wide open, with a two-and-a-half-foot gap.
>
> In the morning when I got up, the living room was cold, the door was open, and my cat, who would normally run outside, was pacing back and forth at the door. It was as if there was an invisible block that was preventing her from going outside. She is an indoor cat and would not know what to do on her own outside. Thank you, angels!

### *Humans' Best Friends—Eternally*

Just like us, our pets' souls never die. Their spirits often stay right by our side following death. I frequently see dogs and cats next to my clients, and I know that they are providing the same sort of love and companionship that they did while alive. The owner may not be consciously aware of their deceased pet's presence, but on a soul level, we know when our dog or cat is there. We benefit by having the pet with us because it adds an extra layer of "love energy" around us—like a moat around a castle or a bumper on a car.

Once after I'd appeared on an East Coast morning show, I walked into the "green room" and saw a 40ish man sitting on a couch. There was a full-color, three-dimensional springer spaniel dog over his right shoulder, reclining in a crescentlike position similar to that old image of the cow jumping over the moon. Normally, I keep my spiritual visions to myself unless someone asks. For some reason, I was impertinent and asked the man, "Did you just recently lose a dog?" His wife, who was also in the green room, rushed to my side in response to my question.

It turned out that their beloved dog had recently died, and we had a beautiful family reunion right there in the green room. The dog showed me scenes of playing with his owners and jumping in piles of colorful autumn leaves with the man. The man and his wife enjoyed reminiscing over these sentimental memories. "I told my dog that we'd always be together," the man shared with me. *They are together,* I thought. *They truly are.*

### The Crystal Elements and Angels

In addition to elementals and animals, the nature kingdom provides us with the "mineral realm" to help us heal. This includes crystals, which have the ability to amplify angelic energy, just as the crystals in watches and radios amplify other forms of energy.

I've found that crystals are a wonderful tool for connecting with the angelic realm. They act like megaphones by increasing the signal strength of communications and healing energies that our angels are sending us. Many of the crystals have properties that are particularly aligned with the angelic realm, including:

**Clear quartz**—Try wearing a clear quartz crystal on a necklace, or holding one up to the area between your two physical eyes ("the third eye"). You'll feel a sensation similar to chills or an air pressure change, which means that the crystal is directing the angelic energy to you like a prism.

**Rose quartz**—A wonderful crystal for opening the heart chakra, which is the center from which we feel love. The more your heart chakra opens, the more you will be open to receiving the outpouring of Divine love that God and the angels bestow upon you.

**Sugalite**—This beautiful purple stone is often called "The Love Crystal" because it elicits a wonderful feeling of high-level love. I find that it is completely aligned with Archangel Michael's energy. The first time I wore a sugalite necklace pendant, I was giving a speech in Colorado Springs. During the speech, I channeled a powerful message from Archangel Michael even though I hadn't planned to do so. Sugalite is wonderful for opening the throat chakra so that you can communicate more clearly and powerfully.

**Amethyst**—This beautiful purple crystal has an extremely high vibration, and some people find that amethysts give them a "buzz" similar to caffeine (so, not everyone can work with amethysts). However, it is a powerful crystal for opening the crown chakra, which is the energy base for "claircognizance," or "clear knowing." It will help you to more clearly receive information from the Universal mind of God, or the collective unconscious.

**Moonstone**—A beautiful opal-like stone that helps you increase your spiritual frequency and vibratory rate. It can also help you better connect with the high energy level of the angelic realm. Its color looks like the transparent beauty of angels.

**Lapis**—A royal-blue stone that is useful in awakening clairvoyance, or the ability to see the nonphysical world and higher dimensions.

**Spectrolite** (AKA **Labradorite**)—This beautiful greenish-blue stone reminds me of the richest colors in mother-of-pearl. It is wonderful in raising the frequency of your intuition and giving an angel's-eye view of all situations. In this way, you can rise above lower-self beliefs and see things from a higher perspective.

### *Angelic Prayers for Animals*

Here are some prayers that you can use with animals. Please rewrite the prayers to fit your particular circumstance and to include your pet's name.

### PRAYER FOR HEALING A PET

*Dear God,*
*I ask that You, Archangel Raphael, and the healing angels surround my pet with Your healing love energy. Please help my pet and me to feel peace so that healing may occur. Please send us a miracle, knowing that everything is already healed in Your eyes. I ask that You help me have faith and trust so that I may experience Your love within my pet and within myself right now. Thank You.*

### PRAYER FOR A LOST PET

*Dearest God,*

*I know that no one and nothing can truly ever be lost, since You are omnipresent and can see everything and everyone. I affirm that nothing is lost in the eyes of God. I ask that You, Archangel Michael, Archangel Raphael, the nature angels, and my guardian angels help me reunite with my pet right now. I call upon the guardian angels of my pet to send a signal so that I may find my pet. I now relax, knowing that God, the angels, and my higher self are already communing with my pet. Thank You.*

# CHAPTER SEVEN

# Angels, Afterlife, and Healing from Grief

Even though the angels know that nobody truly dies, they still empathize with the grief that we endure when a loved one passes away. The angels are here to help us heal from grief, sometimes by showing us signs such as butterflies, birds, or angel-shaped clouds. Other times, our deceased loved ones will deliver a message to us, letting us know that they are okay. As with any life challenge, it's important that we invite our angels to help us heal from painful losses. After all, as mentioned previously, our angels can only intervene when we give them permission.

Our deceased loved ones often function as guardian angels. Those who are recently deceased are with us off and on while they go through experiences similar to school in the afterlife plane. They are always within earshot, so if you mentally call to specific deceased loved ones, they will come to your side right away. Deceased loved ones help us during crises, and they attend holiday and family gatherings. They love to be acknowledged, so even if you're not sure whether that really is the presence of your loved one that you're sensing, say, "Hello, I love you" to them anyway.

Deceased loved ones often enter our dreams to give us angelic healing messages. These dreams are larger than life, with vivid colors and strong emotions. You *know* that they are real experiences, but your lower self may try to convince you that it was your imagination. It wasn't. The angels and our deceased loved ones enter our dreams with healing messages because they know we are wide open to guidance at that time.

### *Saying Good-bye*

Michelle Mordoh Gross, who lives in Spain, related this touching story to me of how an angel helped her say "good-bye" to her dying mother:

> I sat there by my mother's bedside, desperately trying to comfort her, talking to her about life after death and telling her how much I loved her. Doctors could not understand why and how she was holding on to life so long. But *I* did. She wanted to hold on while I was there, until the end of her strength, wanting to spend as much time with me as possible.
>
> So it occurred to me that I was no longer of any help. On the contrary, I was involuntarily forbidding her to leave. It was a brutal revelation; still, I made the hardest decision in my life. I had to leave her so she would feel free to pass on.
>
> I visualized that I was leaving her under the care of an angel. I knew we were spending our last moments together as I held her weakened hand in mine. With a broken heart yet still talking sweetly, I told her about the angel who would be sitting where I was the moment I left. I described the most beautiful angel anyone had ever seen. I told her the angel would come to keep her company, a light in the dark. It would protect, guide, and hold her. I asked her to not be afraid, but to trust.

Tears streamed down my face as she, not able to speak anymore, squeezed my hand in acceptance. I kissed her hand, thanking her for being the bond God chose for me between heaven and earth. And so I left.

It was five P.M., a few hours later, and I was on an airplane headed home. I suddenly opened my eyes from a nap and looked out the window. The sky was bright and blue, cloudless except for a single yellow-and-orange cloud right before my eyes. It had the shape of the beautiful angel I had imagined for my mother, with wings and all! Its arms, extended before it, were holding another cloud in the shape of a person, like a mother holding a sleeping child. And more, under the person-shaped cloud, stood yet another cloud, shaped like a bed. I then knew that my mother was safely on her way home to heaven.

Two hours later, I reached my home, certain that the phone would ring—and it did! Hospital nurse told me the news I already knew. My mom had passed away at five P.M. that day. My mother is now safe—without fear, sickness, or suffering.

During our last conversation, my mother had asked me, "When will *they* come and get me?"

"When you are ready, that is the best time," was my reply. She then promised to send me a rainbow if what I believed was also true for her. And, believe it or not, eight months later, there is not a single day I haven't seen a rainbow, shining bright, and bringing color into my life.

### Family Members on the Other Side

Many of the angels who help us are actually deceased loved ones. They are either permanently assigned to us as "spirit guides" or are with us temporarily during crossroads or crises in our lives. One of the joys of my sessions are the family reunions, where my clients realize that a beloved deceased relative is still with them.

**Doreen**: Your loving and giving nature has attracted many beings on the other side who are ready to help you. You have two deceased female loved ones with you. One of the women with you looks like she colored her hair, she's heavier-set, her face is rounder, and she wasn't elderly when she passed on—perhaps in her '60s. This woman looks like she is of an ethnic descent with darker skin.

**Abby**: Oh, that would be my grandmother on my dad's side! She *did* color her hair, she did have a round face, and was semi-voluptuous. You're describing her exactly.

**Doreen**: Yes, she's with you.

**Abby**: Oh, that's wonderful! We were very close when she was living, and I've missed her so much after her death.

**Doreen**: You've also got a man with you who appears to be a grandfather. He looks like he was a blue-collar dresser. He's tall and big, and he's on your mother's side of the family.

**Abby**: Maybe that's my grandfather who I actually did know, my mother's dad?

**Doreen**: He's handsome, with white hair, like a Bob Barker type.

**Abby**: Yes! Oh, I've got shivers. I've forgotten about him, but I'm so glad that he's there with me!

**Doreen**: He's with you right now. Did you lose a little brown dog, because there's one hanging around you?

**Abby**: Yes, that's my dog, Figi, whom I lost two months ago! Oh, she's with me!

**Doreen**: Yes, she's with you right now, acting as an angel.

ob ob ob

Abby was thrilled to know that her favorite people and dog surrounded her. Once she understood that they were her angels, she began having mental conversations with them regularly. Abby frequently asks her grandma and grandpa to help her, and she reports that she is very grateful for their assistance.

### *Healing Conversations from Beyond*

It's also very meaningful to me when my clients' deceased loved ones send messages to try and heal or improve their post-death relationships. This is one of the ways our deceased loved ones function in angelic ways to help ease our souls of grief or guilt. In the following case, you'll read how my client's deceased sister came through to complete some unfinished business. When we have conversations with our deceased loved ones, we help them ease their souls and bring peace to ourselves in the process.

**Doreen**: There's a woman with you who wasn't that old when she passed.

**Ruth**: Could be my sister.

**Doreen**: Did she have darker hair?

**Ruth**: Yes.

**Doreen**: Okay, then, that's her. There's a sisterly look and feel to her. She looks as if she was in her 50s when she passed.

**Ruth**: She was 52.

**Doreen**: Okay, so that's definitely her. She's very healthy now, I can assure you. Her face is very full, and she's not in any pain. She apologizes because she feels that she was almost sponging off you at the very end of her life.

**Ruth**: Oh, that's so sweet of her, but really, I didn't mind caring for her at all.

**Doreen**: Well, she says that she needs to get this off her chest because it's bothered her since her death. Your sister says that she felt very useless and powerless and that you know she wouldn't have imposed on you unless she absolutely had to.

**Ruth**: Please tell her that it was my pleasure to be with her during her final months.

**Doreen**: She can hear you, Ruth, and she's nodding appreciatively at your words.

**Ruth**: I love you, Sis! I'll always love you.

My client Karla also received a message from the other side that lifted the guilt she'd carried for five years:

**Karla**: My mother passed away five years ago. At the time, I was heavily into drugs. As she was dying, she asked me if I still used drugs and I said no. I lied. I have felt guilty ever since the day she died because of this lie. I only did it because I didn't want to put any more on her than her illness already had. My question is: Does she know I lied? If she does, does she forgive me for it? I am in recovery now, and I have four years, eight months, and eighteen days clean and sober. However, this really bothers me *a lot*.

**Doreen**: Please rest your conscious, dear one. Your mother knows that you told her this because of your love for her and that you were trying to save her from additional stress and pain. She does not judge you in any way—quite the opposite! She blesses you for your caring nature.

Soon after she passed over, she helped you to become clean and sober. She still watches over you with unconditional love, as does your grandmother and two guardian angels.

### *Healthy Relationships with Deceased Loved Ones*

Our relationships with our loved ones don't end with their death. The relationship merely changes form. As a psychotherapist and clairvoyant medium, I help my clients maintain healthy relationships with their loved ones on the other side. Healthy post-death relationships are important for the sakes of souls on both sides of the veil of death.

Grieving survivors have mixed emotions that they must sort through following the death of a loved one. The survivor probably feels a great deal of sadness, loneliness, and confusion. These are feelings that we expect of someone who has just lost a friend or family member. However, survivors sometimes feel anger or a sense of betrayal toward their deceased loved one. These feelings are difficult to work through since most survivors don't like to admit they are angry with someone who has passed away. It doesn't feel "correct" to hold resentment toward someone who is gone.

Yet, admitting these perfectly normal feelings is an important part of healing from a loss. After all, our deceased loved ones are completely aware of how we feel and think about them. We can't hide anything from a person on the other side! We can only hide feelings from ourselves—but at the expense of our peace of mind. When we deny our true feelings, we block our own happiness and also the spiritual progress of our deceased loved one.

My client Laura, for example, was very angry with her father for not taking better care of himself. Laura's dad had passed away after a lengthy illness, and she was furious at him for his unhealthy lifestyle of smoking and drinking, which had contributed to his death. Simultaneously, Laura felt guilty for being angry with her father. She felt she should "have more respect for the dead."

During our first session, Laura's father came through from the other side and asked for Laura to please forgive him. He explained that his deep concern for Laura's emotional welfare was keeping him earthbound. This is a very common occurrence: When we are extremely upset about a loved one's death, he or she stays near us to ensure that we are okay. However, unless our deceased loved one has an assignment to be our spirit guide, spending so much time with us thwarts their own progress. Laura's father wanted to move on to the spirit world so he could participate in growth-producing activities, but he first wanted her permission to leave her side.

Another client, Maryann, held very deep resentment toward her deceased father for the childhood abuse he had inflicted upon her. During our session, Maryann's father came through and expressed his deep regret for hurting her. He also asked for her forgiveness.

As Maryann sobbed tears of grief connected to both her childhood abuse and to her father's death, Maryann's deceased paternal grandfather suddenly appeared. Her grandfather explained that he had been responsible for much of Maryann's childhood abuse. He explained how he had severely beaten Maryann's father when he was a boy. This childhood abuse had spurred Maryann's father into becoming a child abuser when he grew up. The grandfather begged Maryann to forgive him and her father. He explained that by forgiving both of them, Maryann would release herself from the snares of unhealed anger and resentment.

Both Laura and Maryann wanted to forgive their deceased fathers. But wanting to forgive, and honestly forgiving are two separate processes. Both of my clients had several counseling sessions with me before they were ready to release their anger and resentment completely.

Laura was finally able to see her father's unhealthy habits as his way of dealing with his unsatisfying career. She could feel compassion for him for being stuck in a job he didn't like, and this mind-set helped her release her unforgiveness toward him. My other client, Maryann, forgave her father and grandfather after she told me, "I'll forgive my dad and my grandpa, but I won't forgive their acts." This is one way to let go of old anger. After all, it's most important to forgive the person, if not their actions.

We do ourselves and our deceased loved ones a world of good when we openly admit and work through all of our grief-related emotions. One productive method is to write a very honest letter to your deceased loved one. As you write your letter, don't edit or censor your feelings in any way. Remember, your loved one already knows everything you feel about him or her. Your loved one doesn't judge you for holding any negative feelings; he or she simply wants you to feel the peace of mind and happiness that stem from self-honesty and forgiveness.

Your relationships with your loved ones on the other side can be wonderfully fulfilling. Many of my clients tell me that their post-death relationships with their loved ones are even closer and more honest than before their death. Death doesn't mean an end to the love you have shared. Remember: Love never dies!

ॐ ॐ ॐ

Here is a prayer to help you heal from grief and to feel the comfort that your deceased loved one and God want for you. Please edit this prayer so that it comes from your heart and fits your particular situation.

### ANGELIC PRAYER FOR HEALING GRIEF

*Dear God,*

*I know that my deceased loved one is home in heaven with You. I ask that You watch over him/her so that he/she is uplifted by Your love. Please send extra angels to my loved one and help him/her feel wonderful and happy in adjusting to being in heaven. Please send extra angels to my side, and help me release my sadness and grief. Help me heal from my feelings of heaviness so that I may return to the life that I know my loved one wants for me. Please send me a sign from heaven so that I know my loved one is in Your hands. Amen.*

# CHAPTER EIGHT

# How the Angels Help Us in the Material World

I'm often asked if it's okay to ask the angels for help with material issues. "Is it all right if I ask them for a great parking
space?" "Am I wasting the angels' time by asking them to help
me with something that I could easily do myself?" and "Maybe
God will be offended if I ask Him for material items or trivial
things." These are among the concerns I commonly hear, expressing fears that prevent us from asking for help.

The angels repeatedly say to me, *"Matter doesn't matter."*
God and the angels don't perform in a "triage fashion" like doc-
tors who have to judge which person has the most pressing needs.
For one thing, God and the angels have no time and space limitations, so they are able to help everyone simultaneously.

It is also God's will that the angels help us fulfill our higher
self's purpose. God and the angels know that if our minds and
schedules are occupied with worries, concerns, and fears about
material goods or supply, we won't have the time or energy to ful-

fill our purpose. It's not that the angels are here to help us achieve a lifestyle of the rich and famous; they just want to ease our mind so that we are free.

They also know that we sometimes use material items as a time-wasting device that I call a delay tactic. This means any activity that diverts your attention away from fulfilling your purpose.

So, the angels swoop in to alleviate our overinflated concerns with material situations and items. Please don't misunderstand. They don't rescue us from being irresponsible. We wouldn't grow and learn if that was the case. What God and the angels want us to know is this: *"If you need anything, please don't hesitate to call on us to help you. Surrender any situation to us that is causing you distress or making you lose your peace of mind. We promise that we will comfort you and affect the material world in a way that will support you in your present environment. Leave it to us to take you home."* By home, they mean heaven on earth— our natural state, where all of our material supplies are met in Divine order while we focus solely on giving to the world with our natural talents and interests.

### Easing Your Way

When working with the angels, one of the first "tasks" they may assign you is to clear your home, office, or car of clutter. The angels say that our possessions weigh us down and that so much of our focus is on acquiring and then protecting them.

If you've been feeling lately that it's time to donate or discard your unused clutter, then consider this paragraph additional validation. From an energetic standpoint, your living and working environment will feel much cleaner and more efficient without excessive objects.

A good rule of thumb is to lose any item you haven't used for the past two years. Most domestic violence and homeless shelters would be happy to receive your unwanted goods. You'll feel great if you schedule a Saturday afternoon for a massive clean-out day.

By giving away items, you automatically invoke the Spiritual Law of giving and receiving. This means that new items will come to you, and then it will be up to your discernment whether you're simply replacing old clutter with new. A wonderful idea is to keep the circulation going by giving away something every day.

### The Energy of Your Possessions

After you've cleared out unused possessions, you will feel considerably lighter and more organized. The angels will next help you clear the energy in the room through a process known, logically, as "clearing."

Kirlian photographs show that material objects are affected by the thoughts of humans who are in their vicinity. One series of remarkable Kirlian photographs featured a coin that was held by the same person, who deliberately held various emotions. The coin was photographed after the person holding it had angry thoughts. Then, the same coin was photographed when the person held it with loving thoughts. The next photograph captured the coin after the person holding it had fearful thoughts. Each photograph shows a significant change in the size, shape, and color of the "aura" or energy field around the coin.

Kirlian photography is controversial, and scientists cannot agree exactly "what" the camera is capturing. Nonetheless, these photos do document a significant shift occurring as a function of the thoughts of the person holding the coin.

Objects do tend to retain the fingerprint of their owner's dominant thoughts and feelings. This is one reason why I never purchase items from distress sales. I know that the objects retain the energy of the store owner's emotional pain and beliefs about finances. I'd rather pay full price for an object that retains a prosperous store owner's optimism.

## *Psychometry*

When I teach people how to do angel readings, we'll frequently begin by having audience members pair up and face each other in chairs. I then ask the partners to exchange metal objects such as a ring or watch with each other. By holding a person's metal possession, you more easily receive impressions and messages from their guardian angels. We call this method "psychometry."

You can try this yourself by holding someone's keys, watch, or ring in the hand you normally don't write with. This is your "receiving hand," as it absorbs energy. The hand you normally write with is your "sending hand," which gives off energy. So, holding the object in your receiving hand, close your eyes and take a few deep breaths. Hold the intention of talking to your guardian angels and also the guardian angels of the other person. Ask these angels any question such as, "What would you like me to know about (fill in the person's first name)?" or "What message would you like me to deliver to (name)?" or a more specific question.

Then, take a deep breath and notice any impressions that come to you: a feeling, a mental image, a thought, or words. If the other person is with you, begin telling them what impressions you receive. As you talk, you will receive other messages. This is a basic method for giving an angel reading, one that most people can do successfully the first or second time.

## *Clearing Your Space*

Just as objects speak volumes to us, so does the environment in which we live, work, and drive. The walls, floors, and furniture retain the energy of our dominant mind-set. So, if we or our family members are usually in a peaceful frame of mind, our house will reflect that peacefulness. It will be a sanctuary-like setting that anyone who walks in will notice and enjoy.

However, if you or the people who live with you have been involved in arguments or worries, the home's energy will retain the echoes of those problems. Just as furniture, walls, and carpeting absorb the smell of smoke, so do these objects absorb people's psychic stress.

So, your home, office, or vehicle may be retaining the energy fingerprints of everyone who has ever spent time there. For instance, your home may have absorbed negative energy from people who lived there before you did. Fortunately, you can clear your living and driving environment, and the angels will help you do so.

Here are some ways to clear any location, whether it's a home, car, store, or office:

1. Paint the walls.

2. Replace the carpeting.

3. Shampoo the carpeting.

4. Burn some sage-weed (available as incense or on a stick at any metaphysical bookstore). Hold the sage-weed incense or stick, and walk around the environment so that the smoke is distributed throughout the place.

5.  Place a shallow bowl with either salt water or rubbing alcohol in the middle of each room you want cleared.

6.  Place a clear quartz crystal in the middle of each room you want cleared. Make sure that the crystal is first cleared of old energy by placing it in direct sunlight or moonlight for at least four hours.

7.  Ask Archangel Michael and his helpers, known as the "band of mercy," to enter and circle your environment. Michael and the angels will escort any negative energies away from your home, office, store, or vehicle.

### Manifesting a Home

If you desire a new home, the angels can help you find the perfect living place. They will also open doors to smooth the way so that you can easily afford to move. One thing the angels have taught me is to release the human doubts that say, "Well, it's just not possible because it's illogical." The angels rise above human logic to an elevation where all things are possible.

A couple from Virginia named Martha and Stan discovered the miracles that are possible when we let go of doubt:

> *Martha and Stan, married ten years, dearly wanted to own a home. Martha, a woman of great faith, said prayers each evening and asked God and Jesus to help her and her husband find a residence that would be filled with love, and that would also be affordable. One evening she had a clear dream in which she toured an older house with Grandma-like charm: lace curtains; wooden floors; and in the upstairs bathroom, a beautiful basin sink with golden roses painted on the ceramic fin-*

ish. Martha remembers that in her dream she felt quite at home, and she knew that she wanted to live there.

The dream was so beautiful and vivid that Martha described it in detail to Stan the next morning. The couple took the dream as a sign that it was time to look for their house. So they contacted a Realtor and began house-hunting. Two weeks into their search, as the three of them toured a house, Martha caught her breath and loudly whispered to Stan, "I think this is the house I dreamed about!" An unexplained familiarity washed over Martha, and Stan got goose bumps at the thought.

As the couple entered the upstairs bathroom, they caught sight of the one detail that had so vividly stood out in Martha's dream: golden roses painted on the ceramic sink basin. "This is it!" they both exclaimed, and asked the Realtor to make an offer on the home for them.

The owner readily accepted their offer, and the couple excitedly filled out the home loan application. The day after they applied for the loan, however, Stan was laid off from his job. Since Martha didn't work, the couple was initially dejected. "How can we ever qualify for a loan without a source of income?" they wondered. So, they prayed for help and surrendered the whole matter to God, saying, "If it's God's will, we will have the house."

Within two days, Stan was hired as a commission-only salesman. The couple immediately informed the bank loan officer, who dourly exclaimed, "Well, since Stan has no track record as a salesperson, I doubt that this loan will go through. I've never seen the V.A. approve a loan unless there's a steady source of consistent income."

The bank officer was thinking on a human level and probably wasn't aware of the influence that prayers have on situations such as home-shopping. She was dumb-

*struck when she called Stan and Martha the following day and said, "I don't believe it. They approved your loan!" The couple hugged and happily moved into their home with the golden rose sink.*

ᘛ ᘛ ᘛ

Over the years since I've been interviewing people about Divine intervention, this sort of story has become almost commonplace in my files. I've talked to dozens, perhaps hundreds, of people who have actively asked for spiritual help in selling their home, locating a new home, obtaining a loan, affording the rent or mortgage, and moving. Their stories are consistent: If you ask for help, you receive it in miraculous ways.

### Shopping with the Angels

The angels intervene in our material world with great joy. We never need to be shy in asking for their assistance, or worry that our request is too trivial or unimportant. We must remember that the angels are here to smooth our path so that we are free to shine God's bright light. We all know that we shine brighter on days when things go our way. We stand taller, smile bigger, and are more optimistic when we're "on a roll." These are also the days when we inspire others to reach for their own stars. So, let's not hesitate to ask heaven to help us to have these kinds of days more often!

The angels love to open doors for us. We can ask for their guidance in locating needed items, and then "listen" for their guidance, which always follows a request for help. The guidance may come through a thought, vision, feeling, or voice.

An interior decorator told me how the angels helped her locate an item that her client wanted for her home:

One of my clients needed some accessories to finish a newly designed bedroom. I'd been searching for an alabaster lamp, one of her most desired items, for four months. On the way into an antique shop, I called on the angels to lead us to just what we needed and desired. Moments later, we found not only one alabaster lamp, but two, as well as some other elusive nightstands and accessories we required. It was easy, fun, and took hardly any time at all to shop with the angels.

A woman I know named Gail Wiggs had a similar experience. Every spring and fall, she attends a Phoenix arts-and-crafts fair. She looks forward to purchasing the fair's theme T-shirts, as they always feature a beautiful original silk-screen painting on the front. In the fall, she purchases a long-sleeved T-shirt. However, these shirts are extremely popular, and they sell out rapidly. So, Gail makes a point to go early to the fair so she is sure to find one. However, last fall, her busy schedule wouldn't allow her to go to the fair until quite late. She asked her angels to be sure to save her a long-sleeved T-shirt.

It was afternoon by the time Gail took a shuttle bus to the fair. The bus stopped at an unfamiliar entrance, and the driver announced that it was the last stop. Gail entered the fair at this place—a different one than she usually used—but as soon as she entered, there was an information booth with the theme T-shirts in front of her.

There was one long-sleeved theme T-shirt left—a large—which she promptly purchased. Gail checked every other information booth as she went through the fair and rapidly discovered that no other long-sleeved T-shirts were left. Gail thanked her angels, and for the next two months she began getting strong messages that she was supposed to start a T-shirt company featuring images of angels on the shirts. Gail is currently starting such a business, and she is filled with joy to be able to market items that have brought her so much joy in the past.

## *Be Careful What You Ask For!*

My husband, Michael, and I were at the airport, walking to the baggage claim area to get our four big suitcases, filled with supplies for my weekend workshop. It was late on a Friday night, and we were hungry for dinner.

I said to Michael, "Let's ask Raphael, the archangel of healers and travelers, to get the luggage off the plane right away." I then hesitated, because I knew the importance of being careful about what you ask for. If you're going to specify to the angels what you want, you better make sure to fill in all the blanks of your request carefully. So I edited my request to Raphael, "I don't mean for you to get the luggage so quickly that they fall onto the tarmac. Just please have them be on the luggage carousel right away."

I thought I was covering all of my bases with this request, but the angels taught me how they take our requests literally. As I walked away from the carousel to rent a big luggage cart, I heard Michael's voice calling for help. I turned around and saw that all four of our suitcases had come down the luggage chute simultaneously. Unfortunately, since they came out together, Michael couldn't grab them all at once. So, we waited while our bags made their trip all the way around the large carousel at the international airport. We both had the same thought: "Next time we'll be more careful about what we ask for!"

## *The Angels Heal Mechanical Items*

I used to watch my mother pray whenever our family automobile conked out. Amazingly, the engine would always reignite following her affirmative prayers. I've asked for Divine intervention for mechanical and electronic devices ever since.

In particular, Archangel Michael is wonderful at healing broken faxes, washing machines, and other mechanical items. I've called on him when I'm having computer glitches, and I've had the situation immediately resolved.

A spiritual counselor named Johanna Vandenberg had a similar happy outcome when she requested that Michael help her with some plumbing:

> My godson's mother had asked me to change her water filter since she was extremely busy with lots of chores. Alone in her apartment, I attempted to perform the task. It looked so simple: a sinktop domed filter—just unscrew the bottom, put in a new cartridge, and put the bottom back on again. However, I couldn't get the bottom off—it was stuck!
>
> After 45 minutes, I finally got it loose, put in the new cartridge, and screwed on the bottom. I then turned on the water, as it's supposed to run for 15 minutes before use. But all the water began dripping out of the bottom of the filter! I took off the bottom again, put it back on, water dripping, over and over, until I was cursing. The family was coming home soon, and I felt pressured to have it repaired before they returned.
>
> At this desperate moment, I suddenly held up my hands and yelled, "St. Michael and Raphael, please help me put in this water filter!" I took the bottom off, put it back on again, turned on the water, and it worked perfectly! Everything was fixed within 90 seconds! Later, I got a call from my godson's Mom, who thanked me profusely and said the filtered water is coming out about ten times the force it usually does, and how did I get it that way?
>
> I was about to throw the thing out the window, feeling so frustrated trying to fix it for about an hour and a half. Yet the angels helped me so easily, so quickly, and so beautifully! As a result, there is now clean water for that family.

So, calling upon archangels is a very effective way of getting yourself out of jams involving material objects. Other people, such as Sharon, a psychotherapist I know, prefer to call upon their personal guardian angels whenever they need assistance. No call for help goes unanswered, and you can't get a "wrong number" when you put out a call for help to heaven. Sharon's guardian angel recently helped her "heal" her vehicle:

> The heater on my Jeep was out. As I drove to work Monday morning I felt the strong presence of an angel in my passenger seat. I asked what her name was, and I heard an inner voice say, *"Angela."*
>
> I had asked for angels to guard my home and Jeep several months prior, and I felt her say that she was the angel who had been guarding my Jeep since I first asked for angelic protection for it. I asked her to contact whoever the angel was who repairs Jeep heaters, because mine has been out for about two weeks. I received an impression in my gut as if Angela had said she would do that. The very next evening, my heater started working again!

# CHAPTER NINE

# Spiritual Safety with the Angels

In truth, the world is a 100 percent safe place to live. However, it appears to be a dangerous place because of the thought-forms of fear that act like reflections of any worry or apprehension we've carried in our minds. Because we sometimes miscreate with our thoughts, the angels help to guard and protect us.

### Protector Angels

God and the angels ensure that we and everything we own are safe and protected. Of course, this still means that we have to ask for their help and then listen to and follow the guidance that we receive. My friend Mary Ellen discovered this rule in a dramatic—and near-tragic—way:

She and her friend Nancy, both American college students in their 20s, were on a strictly budgeted vacation in Germany. They were hitchhiking across the countryside, which was a cultural norm at the time. Two U.S. army trucks stopped to pick up the two women, and they each got in separate trucks. I'll let Mary Ellen tell the rest of the story in her own words:

> The driver of the truck I was in had rather unethical intentions. He started to attack me. I was thinking as fast as I could and praying for help to thwart his advances. I told this young New York soldier that I was not that kind of woman. And he said he didn't care. Just then, an invisible male voice out side of my left ear, very audibly to me said, *"Tell him you will tell."*
>
> I didn't think that would work, so I said, "How would you like your sister to come to Europe and make love to a stranger?" I figured he would see that she would not do that and neither would I.
>
> The invisible male voice out side of my left ear repeated, *"Tell him you will tell."* I thought that would be a nutty thing to say and that it would not possibly deter any attacker.
>
> The funny part now is that I never thought it odd to hear the voice. Maybe if I had said, "Do you hear that little voice?" the soldier would have thought I was crazy and left me alone!
>
> So, I said, "If you don't get off of me, I will pull my knife on you." Now, this sounded tough, but I had a knife for my bread-and-cheese picnic. "That won't bother me." He then pulled up his shirtsleeves and showed knife marks all up and down his arms from New York street fights.
>
> I thought, *Uh-oh.*
>
> The male voice outside my left ear screamed, *"TELL HIM YOU WILL TELL!"* I thought, *Sheesh, if a knife won't work, why would that statement?*
>
> But I had nothing left to say, so I said, "I'll tell."
>
> Well, this guy leaped off of me. I was so stunned. He said, "You wouldn't!"
>
> And my brain is thinking, *Here I am in a country where I don't speak the language, I don't have anyone to call or tell, and I did not even know where we were.*

So I said, "Yes, I will tell."

He started the truck and in silence drove me to the depot where the other truck was with Nancy. She was worried about me and glad to see me drive up. I never told her about the voice, but I know that I was saved by God, the angels, and my prayers for protection.

I had a similar experience, also with a happy outcome. I was exercising on a rooftop area that had a treadmill. About halfway into my workout, I noticed a man sitting in a car across the street. It appeared that he was staring up at me, and I felt a creepy feeling, as if I were his prey.

At first I tried to ignore or rationalize the situation. After all, why would someone stare at me? I was dressed very conservatively, with a baggy sweatshirt, loose sweatpants, and no make-up. Yet, my intuition said that this man was staring at me with dishonorable intentions.

I had two choices: I could stop exercising and leave, or I could try a spiritual approach. I opted for the latter. Mentally, I held the intention of talking with this man's guardian angels. I told them that this man was frightening me, and would they please ask him to leave? I felt a sense of peace, and about three minutes later, I heard his engine ignite and gratefully watched him drive away.

One week later, a woman approached me and said that she had noticed this man staring at me on three different occasions. She gave me his license plate number since his behavior had alerted her. However, after that day when I had a discussion with his angels, no one ever saw him again!

## *Road Protection*

The angels protect us in many ways. Sometimes the slow driver ahead of us is an angel in disguise. A woman I'll call Rebecca related this story to me about just such an angel:

> I once had a guy pull out in front of me from a parking space while I was driving through a small city where I once worked. His car was driving a little slower than I would have driven. Then, as we approached an intersection, a car zoomed right through a red light (we still had a green light). If I hadn't been cut off by the guy pulling out from the parking space, I would have been in the middle of that intersection when the car ran its red light, and I don't think I'd be here today!

Heaven also protects us in ways that defy Earthly laws. For example, if your car is running low on fuel, the angels will make sure that you reach your destination safely. For instance, they'll help you keep driving until you reach a gas station, even if you're out of fuel. Or, if you *do* run out of gas, the angels will send a rescuer to your aid quickly.

Miriam, an elderly woman I interviewed, told me that she was stuck on the side of a desolate road with a flat tire one afternoon. Unsure of how to change a tire, she prayed for assistance. Within moments, a man and woman walked up to her and offered to help. As the couple changed Miriam's tire, she noticed that they had simply "appeared" without a car. There were no buildings from which the couple could have emerged. After the new tire was on the car, the couple vanished as mysteriously as they had appeared. As a psychologist, I knew that Miriam was a lucid and intelligent adult who wasn't hallucinating or exaggerating as she told me this story.

Acting like superheroes, the angels are also able to affect physical matter to avert accidents. Karen Noe, a spiritual coun-

selor from New Jersey, tells the following remarkable story of
how the angels saved the day:

> My eight-year-old son, Timmy, and I were in a supermar-
> ket parking lot on an extremely steep hill. A very busy street
> with four lanes of traffic is at the bottom of this hill. As we
> headed for my car, I saw a shopping cart rolling very fast down
> the hill, heading straight for the busy road. If it had continued
> at this rate, it would have gone into the street and would have
> definitely caused an accident!
>
> As I saw it going down the hill, I immediately said, "God,
> please stop that cart . . . now!" The cart stopped right then and
> there, *in the middle of the hill, on an incline*! There was no one
> in the section of the parking lot where the cart stopped! Then,
> a man came out of nowhere and moved the cart in the other
> direction on top of a parking bump so that it couldn't roll any-
> more, and as I turned my head to tell my son to look what was
> happening, the "man" literally disappeared!
>
> My son is so accustomed to us calling on the angels for
> everything that he just said, "It's an angel again," as though he
> has seen this kind of thing every day (which he does).

Karen's request for help, coupled with the unwavering faith
that she and her son held, created this miracle. All we need to do
is ask, and then have some inkling of faith—even if the faith is
fleeting. Still, I want to say that when people do experience tragic losses, it doesn't mean that God or the angels has abandoned
them. Losses occur for many reasons, including the fact that it
may be someone's time to go. Yet, I always believe that when we
ask for help and listen to it when it comes, the angels help us to
either escape danger or considerably lessen its effects.

## *White Light*

A wonderful way to ensure the safety and stability of your home and possessions is to surround them with "white light." White light is an angel energy that has a life force and intelligence all its own. When you surround yourself or your possessions with white light, you've put up a shield that ensures its protection.

So, if someone with harmful intentions comes near you or the item surrounded with white light, that person won't be able to cause harm. They will be compelled to leave you and your possessions alone without understanding why they were repelled. In some cases, the person may not even *see* you or your items, almost as if the white light makes objects invisible to people with negative intentions.

It's easy to surround yourself, your loved ones, or your items with white light. Simply close your eyes and visualize white light surrounding the entire outline of the person or object. Imagine what the person or item would look like with an eggshell of white light completely covering them. Once you've been able to see this in your mind's eye, the task is complete!

If fears about burglars or fires keep you awake at night, you'll sleep soundly when you ask the angels to help you. Simply visualize your home surrounded by white light. Next, visualize a large guardian angel posted next to each door, and even each window if you like. With the light and the guardian angels watching over you and your home, you will sleep safe and sound.

You can also surround your children and other loved ones with white light for spiritual insulation. I also like to surround the car or plane that I'm traveling in with white light. I often ask for extra angels to escort and buffer my vehicle as well.

In addition, whenever you walk into a location where any kind of negativity or earthbound mentality exists, surround yourself with white light. If you tend to be clairsentient (also known as empathic, intuitive, or sensitive), you may be prone to absorbing negative energy from these environments. Clairsentient people tend to be acutely aware of other people's feelings, and they can easily soak up others' negativity. The result is that the clairsentient may often feel drained or discouraged.

To prevent these negative emotions, clairsentients might visualize a triple seal of light around themselves: first a layer of white light, followed by a second layer of emerald-green light for healing, and then a layer of purple light. The third layer acts like a bumper that deflects any negative influences.

The angels also say that clairsentients need to spend regular time outdoors. According to the angels, nature acts like a "smoke absorber" and removes negative energies that the clairsentient has taken in. The angels strongly recommend that clairsentients keep potted plants next to their beds, especially broad-leafed plants such as pothos and philodendrons. The plants absorb residue or negativity from the body while one is asleep, much like they remove carbon monoxide from our air.

### *Finding Lost Items*

When I was a young girl, I lost my little coin purse while walking home from school. That night, I cried about my loss, but my mother reassured me by asking me to affirm, "Nothing is lost in the mind of God." She explained that although I didn't know where my purse was, God could see it right at that very moment.

I fell asleep, affirming repeatedly, "Nothing is lost in the mind of God," feeling full faith that God would bring my purse back to me. When I opened my eyes the next morning, there was my little red coin purse, sitting right next to my bed. My mother swore that she had nothing to do with its recovery. To this day, she says the same thing, and I believe it truly was a miracle brought about by my complete faith in God's power.

I've taught that affirmation to many people, and have since

received many letters from people who say they've also experienced miraculous recoveries of lost items by repeatedly affirming, "Nothing is lost in the mind of God."

You can also ask your angels to help you locate lost items. I had just moved into a new home, and my office supplies were in disarray in various boxes. I couldn't find my checks and needed them to pay some bills. I implored my angels, "Please, where are my checks?"

I heard a voice say, *"Check the closet!"*

As I opened the cluttered closet, I felt my attention and hands guided immediately to a large bag. There was my checkbook, exactly where my angel's voice said it would be.

A woman named Jenny had lost her keys, which included the ones to her car, home, and post office box. She and her husband searched everywhere, with no luck. Two days after losing her keys, Jenny and her husband were in their garage talking. She was getting ready to drive to the grocery store, using her husband's car since she had no key to drive her own. She was really upset that she couldn't find her keys, and said aloud to God, "Please help me find my car keys now!" As soon as she'd finished the sentence, Jenny looked at an inverted empty coffee can in the garage. It seemed to glow from within, and she was irresistibly drawn to it. Her husband didn't notice, distracted by his project.

As she picked up the coffee can, Jenny saw the unmistakable glimmer of her car keys beneath it. "How could that be?" she wondered. "I remember looking under the coffee can twice for the keys, and they weren't there before." A woman of great faith, though, Jenny didn't question the miracle that had occurred immediately after she'd asked God for help. Instead, she decided to surprise her husband, who was still preoccupied with his project.

Jenny got into her car and lightly tapped the horn. "Bye, honey, I'm going to the store now!" He absentmindedly waved at her, and as Jenny pulled out of the driveway, he suddenly realized that his wife was driving a car for which she had no keys. He ran after her, and they both laughed as Jenny explained about the Divine guidance that had led her to find them

Heaven also helps us replace ruined items, as spiritual counselor Maria Stephanson, whom you met earlier, discovered:

> I was invited to a black tie event and purchased a stunning blouse for $155 at a very exclusive shop. This was a big thing for me. I am the original "shop for the bargain" person and have never spent more than about $25 for a blouse. It was something I knew I could wear during the holidays and special occasions.
>
> About a month after the event, a very close friend of mine had a formal affair, and, trusting her completely, I let her borrow my blouse. After wearing it, she took it to the cleaners, and it was completely ruined. She was devastated, cried her eyes out, and didn't sleep all night prior to telling me. She had called the cleaners and the shop where I'd purchased it, and they both requested the receipt before they would even attempt to refund the money. She wanted to replace it, but at the shop where I purchased the blouse, it was the only one they had. I felt a little bad, but I actually felt worse for my friend.
>
> Now, my problem was that I could not find the receipt anywhere. I searched high and low for a full day, ripping everything apart and finally had resolved in my mind that this was one more thing I could just say good-bye to. However, I had just attended a one-day workshop with Dr. Virtue and started thinking about how she had given me some ways to communicate with our angels. I also listened to the *Divine Guidance* tapes.
>
> So, I decided to ask my angels, "If, in fact, I do still have this receipt somewhere, could you just show me where?" I immediately got the feeling to check a drawer in my kitchen. The message was so powerful that I spun around on my heels and walked straight to the drawer and opened it, absolutely *knowing* that the receipt would be there. And I was right!
>
> I laughed, gave thanks, and brought the receipt to my

friend. She told me she would take it to the cleaners and get a refund. The next day, she surprised me with the blouse! She had taken a chance and had gone to the shop. They had just gotten one in, and it "just happened" to be my size. They were very kind and replaced it with no questions. So not only did my angels help me find the receipt, but there was a blouse just sitting there waiting for me!

## Lost and Found Money

Of the Divine intervention stories that I receive, some of the more heartwarming ones involve people who lose their purses or wallets and then recover them through miraculous means. These stories not only reaffirm my faith in God and the angels watching over us, but also bolster my faith in the essential goodness of humankind. A counselor named Gayle Earle told the following uplifting story about how her angels and good people helped her find her wallet:

> I accidentally left my wallet in the shopping cart at the grocery store. I went home, unpacked my groceries, and was back in my car on my way to the next store. I asked my angels, "Okay, which store should I go to today for the rest of the stuff I need?" I did not get a clear response, so I felt frustrated. Then I received the message, *"Do you know where your wallet is?"* I realized that I could not find it.
>
> Something compelled me to go back to the grocery store. Sure enough, someone had brought it into the store, and it was waiting there for me, cash and all. Our world is full of loving and honest people, and I am blessed to be a part of it.

In another story of lost and found money, two healers named Rachelle and Mary Lynn asked the Archangel Michael to watch over their missing purse:

*Rachelle and Mary Lynn were driving from Pittsburgh to Cleveland and stopped at a restaurant for dinner. One hour later, they pulled into a gas station. Mary Lynn reached for her purse to pay for the gas, but to her horror, she realized that she'd left it at the restaurant.*

*Since both women have great faith in the power of angels, particularly Archangel Michael, they immediately asked him to watch over Mary Lynn's purse. Then they affirmed, "Everything is in Divine and perfect order" to help anchor their faith.*

*Driving back to the restaurant, they asked their angels for directions to the restaurant since they couldn't remember where it was located. They felt the presence of angels guiding and calming them, and they got off at the right exit, went to the restaurant, and the manager handed Mary Lynn her purse. Everything, including her credit cards and $200 in cash, was intact.*

*One month later, Mary Lynn had to call Archangel Michael in on another case of missing items! Since she is a cardiac nurse, Mary Lynn "floats" through the hospital and doesn't have a permanent desk or locker. She keeps all of her belongings, including keys, money, and day planner, in a briefcase.*

*One night, Mary Lynn was very busy with an emergency, and her briefcase was left unattended. After the surgery, she discovered that it was missing! So, she immediately asked Michael to locate her belongings, plus she sent blessings and Divine love to the person who had taken it. Within one hour, Mary Lynn received a phone call from security, saying that they had her briefcase. As before, all of her belongings were recovered without anything missing.*

❧ ❧ ❧

Whenever we lose any item, it's important to ask for spiritual help. So often I talk to folks who tell me stories of how they searched for hours for an item. Then, they finally ask God and the angels to help them and—boom!—the item is found minutes later. This is what a woman named Maggie discovered as well.

*A part-time waitress and student, Maggie had carefully placed her $65 cash payment from the previous evening's work inside an envelope in her purse. Then she ran some errands during which she took out $5 from the envelope to buy food at a Taco Bell.*

*The next morning, she searched everywhere for the envelope full of money, but it was gone. Maggie searched all through her trash cans and under every paper in the house, spending several hours searching to no avail. Finally, in desperation, she turned to God and the angels for help.*

*The instant she made this request, Maggie received a mental image of the Taco Bell bag from her dinner the night before. She went to the trash can, opened the bag, and there was her envelope full of money!*

### Angelic Reminders

The angels take care of us and our homes as well. A participant in one of my Divine Guidance workshops related this story to me:

As I drove to work the other day, I heard a voice inside my head telling me that the coffeepot was left on. I would normally not think about this at all, as my husband frequently works out of our house, and he's the one who primarily makes and drinks coffee. Yet, the voice sounded imperative.

So I called my husband and got him on his cell phone as

he was driving. I asked him if he'd remembered to turn off the coffeepot before leaving the house. "Oops, I forgot!" he exclaimed. He returned home and turned it off, grateful that the angels were watching over our precious home.

### Angels on the Road

The majority of angel stories that I receive concern automobiles. Our angels closely monitor us when we're in cars because they don't want anything to happen to us before our time. Of course, they can only do so much, such as scream warnings at us. Our free will gives us the option to ignore the angels' pleas to slow down, change lanes, and so forth.

A caller on a radio show asked me about the angels surrounding her. "There's a large female angel standing next to your right shoulder," I said. "She's wiping her brow and showing me that she helps you while driving and has kept you from a number of near misses. She acts like you keep her busy nonstop, saving you while driving. Let me ask you, do you drive like a maniac or something?"

"Well, not exactly," was her demure reply, "but I do put my makeup on while I'm driving to work." I saw an image of this woman driving with her visor mirror in front of her, applying her lipstick while her angel frantically grabbed the steering wheel.

The angels love us, but they want us to pay attention while we're driving!

The following story, told to me by a woman named Lynette, is the most typical type of Divine intervention I hear:

> I was driving in the fast lane when I heard a voice inside my head saying, *"Slow down, now!"* I slowed down a bit, and as soon as I did, a car came out of nowhere. I had to slam on the brakes to avoid hitting the car broadside. I literally stopped six inches from her car! The incredible thing was that I wasn't even

scared or shaking—startled a little, but my knees weren't knocking like I would have expected in a sudden situation such as this.

Many of the stories I hear about Divine intervention are hair-raising tales, such as David's experience.

*David was driving on a busy Southern California freeway when he suddenly noticed his gas gauge needle dropping rapidly from F to E.* Hmm, I just filled the car up with gas, *David thought.* I wonder if I left the gas cap off of the car at the gas station. *As the gas gauge fell below* E *with the reserve light on, David pulled to the side of the freeway to investigate.*

*A moment after he pulled off the side of the road, David heard a huge crash. He looked up, and in the lane he had just exited from was a three-car pile-up. If he hadn't pulled off the road, David surely would have been in the collision!*

*He said a prayer of thanks and also prayed for the people involved in the accident. Then he cautiously stepped out of his car to confirm that his gas cap was on— which it was. David then turned his key in the ignition and was amazed to watch the gas gauge climb immediately to* F. *His reliable car had never had a problem with the gas gauge before, and hasn't since. David knows that God and the angels rescued him from a serious accident by manipulating his gas gauge. They obviously knew David well enough to know that he'd immediately investigate such an occurrence!*

As David's story illustrates, the angels can affect the physical world and create miracles when needed. Madison, a healer from Utah, experienced how angels can defy physics:

> I was driving in the right-hand lane of a four-lane road. There was a car in front of me and one to the left. All of a sudden, the driver in front of me hit his brakes! I had to swerve into the left lane to avoid hitting the car. By all rights, I should have hit the car to my left side. But I looked up in the rear-view mirror and the car that had been on my left was about six car lengths in back of me. There is no doubt in my mind that I was saved by my angels.

## Angelic Time Warps

Many people, myself included, have also discovered that angels can help us reach our destinations on time. One woman said that she was running late in picking a friend up at the airport:

> There was no physical way for me to reach the plane on time, so I asked my angels to help me get there. Somehow, I got to the airport, parked, and was at the gate to meet her with five minutes to spare, and her plane was on time! It was as if the angels helped me to go into a time warp, because the drive to the airport always took one hour, and I made it in 30 minutes. I wasn't speeding or driving any differently than I normally do.

Another woman told me a similar story:

> I was running late and left the house 20 minutes later than I normally do. I asked my angels to get me to work quickly, safely, and without stress. Usually, it takes me between 30 and 40 minutes to get there. Today, I arrived in 15 minutes! There was virtually no traffic, I made all but two stop lights, and at

those, I waited only seconds. I did not exceed the speed limit at all, and I actually arrived at work early! Thank you, angels.

If I hadn't experienced similar miracles of angelic "time warps," I wouldn't believe these stories. But I've had similar things happen to me and have heard so many of these stories that I now accept these events as normal options available to anyone who asks the angels for help in time traveling.

On a less mystical but related note, a woman named Patti told me this story:

> Driving home from a friend's house this evening, I took a route unknown to me. I simply affirmed, "I am Divinely guided," and I felt myself led by an unseen force to take many streets that I'd never before driven on. I actually ended up shaving 15 minutes off my normal commute time from her house to mine!

## Safety at Work

One day I was on a Midwest radio show doing angel readings by phone from my home. I find that I can easily see someone's angels, whether I'm talking with them face-to-face, over the phone, on the radio, or even just by thinking about the person. Our spiritual sight, or clairvoyance, is not limited in the way that our physical sight is.

The caller on the radio show said that he was a firefighter who had narrowly escaped death the previous evening. "Someone helped me to get out of that burning house," he said breathlessly. "I know it! I could feel the presence and hands of someone helping me escape, yet there were no other firefighters in the house with me. I was totally alone, and I know this was an angel who saved my life. I have an idea who it was who saved me, but I just want to make sure. Could you tell me who my guardian angel is?

Who saved my life last night?"

"Yes, it's your grandfather," I said. I had watched the elderly gentleman next to the caller's right side the entire time he was talking. The grandfather showed me how much he adored his grandson and wouldn't let him come into harm's way.

The caller was amazed by the instant validation. "I knew it!" he exclaimed. "My granddad passed away just three months ago. I'm holding his death certificate and photo in my hands right now. I knew he was the one who saved my life! Please tell him I said thank you, okay?"

"He can hear you right now," I replied. "He knows that you are grateful, and he also knows that you love him very much. He loves you, too."

Our angels help us stay safe at work. They'll intervene if we're faced with a life-endangering situation before it's our time to go. The fireman experienced this type of heroics from his granddad, the guardian angel.

However, for day-to-day safety issues, we must give God and the angels permission to intervene. Because of the law of free will, they can only help us if we—or someone who loves us, such as a parent, friend, or spouse—ask for their help.

Police officers consider Archangel Michael their patron saint because he watches over and protects them. Many law enforcement officers wear pins or carry images of Archangel Michael as reminders to ask for his help. Michael's protection is not limited to police officers, however. Like a living Superman, Michael is able to be with everyone simultaneously who asks for his help and protection.

Mentally ask Archangel Michael to stay next to you and guide you. He'll tell you, very loudly and clearly, if you need to get out of harm's way. Michael helps everyone, regardless of their religious or nonreligious orientation. All he asks is that you request his assistance. He'll take care of everything else.

I also find it helpful to visualize work equipment and facilities surrounded with white light. As discussed earlier, white light is a form of angelic energy that has intelligence, power, and life force. When you imagine a piece of work equipment surrounded by white light, it becomes insulated against damage or theft. Use your intuition to know if you need to regularly continue to re-seal it in light, or if the item will stay permanently sealed. If in doubt, re-seal it in white light for extra protection and insulation.

If you are worried about a loved one's safety at work, mentally call for additional angels to surround the person. Visualize your loved one encapsulated in white light. Know that the angels and light will never violate the other person's free will. However, they will create a "moat effect" which will prevent untoward energies from coming into contact with your loved one.

### Peace and Quiet

The angels know that noise is a major stressor that can rattle our nerves, interrupt our sleep, and erode our peace of mind. Fortunately, when we ask for their assistance, the angels are able to intervene and bring heavenly quiet to any situation.

A radio talk show host told me that his guardian angel helped him have a peaceful morning. It was Saturday about seven A.M.., and he was trying to sleep late on his day off. However, the neighbor's dog was barking furiously. *How am I ever going to sleep with this racket?* he thought, annoyed. Then he remembered that I had given him an angel reading on his show the week before. I'd told him that his main guardian angel's name was Horatio, and that he could call upon this angel for help with *anything*. "I figured I'd put Horatio to work helping me," he recalled. "So I mentally said to Horatio, 'Please get that dog to stop barking, right now!' The second I finished making the request, the dog became completely silent and stayed that way all morning long. Count me in as a believer!"

I'm very sensitive to noise because my ears are attuned to hearing angels' voices. So, when I arrived at a seminar location recently and found that the fire alarm was going off (a false alarm), I was determined to heal the situation rapidly. Their fire alarm system consisted of flashing strobe lights on the four corners of the seminar room's walls, accompanied by a very loud, shrill alarm that would sound every two minutes. You could talk at a normal pitch for a couple of minutes and then—oops!—the fire alarm would go off, and everyone would have to yell to be heard. The strobe lights were flashing continuously, creating a weird disco effect.

A few of my students were at the seminar with me, and we all huddled in a circle moments before I was scheduled to begin my lecture. Together, we asked for Archangel Michael and Raphael to fix the fire alarm. I asked for deceased firefighters and engineers to come to our aid and alleviate the situation. Then we turned the entire matter over to God. I felt assured that somehow the fire alarms would be fixed by the time my speech began.

As I was being introduced moments later, the strobe lights suddenly stopped flashing. Everyone looked around as they realized that the fire alarms had been fixed at just the moment I walked onto the stage. Ask and you shall receive!

This worked so well that the following week when I was again accosted by noise, I decided to try this technique once more. I was at the beach, relaxing after an extended period of very hard work. I had maybe two hours to enjoy myself when two young men sat right next to me and turned on their boom box, which was playing loud rap music.

I mentally conversed with the young men's guardian angels, saying, "Please let them know that their music is bothering me, and would they please turn it down?" I knew that the angels would try to help me, but I wasn't so sure whether the young men would listen to their angels or ignore their conscience! Yet, moments later, they turned off their boom box. Asking for angels' help always works.

My manager, Steve Allen, discovered the proof of this when we were filming a segment for a national television show at my home. During the interview, my refrigerator was making a lot of noise. Steve mentally asked his angels to quiet the refrigerator, and the motor shut off the instant he asked! Although Steve is a man of great faith, even he was surprised by how rapidly his request was granted.

# CHAPTER TEN

## Healing Our Past-Life Issues with the Angels

As a therapist, I've always been intrigued by the topic of past lives. For years, however, even though I could see the therapeutic value of conducting cathartic past-life regression sessions, I believed the whole subject was founded in fantasy. Of course, I also didn't believe in angels or life after death for a long time either! I was a left-brained skeptic about all things esoteric. It took a few miracles before I was sufficiently open to the idea of a spirit world.

Still, even when I thought that the idea of past lives was nonsense, I saw its therapeutic value. Many clients with phobias didn't heal until they underwent past-life regressions—for example, a woman who compulsively overate and didn't respond to traditional therapy. Yet, when she underwent hypnosis with the intention of finding the original trauma connected with her compulsion, she saw in her mind's eye a scenario where she had starved to death in a previous life. Immediately following the session, her appetite normalized and she dropped weight.

Now, does it really matter whether the woman actually had the past life or not? No! The only practical consideration is the here-and-now, since healing can only occur in the present moment.

In my book *Divine Guidance: How to Have a Dialogue with God and Your Guardian Angels*, I discuss practical ways to clearly receive advice and suggestions from heaven. Yet, hearing the advice isn't enough. We've got to follow it, to put Divine guidance into action. If you're feeling stuck, paralyzed in your ability to apply Divine guidance to your everyday life, it could be because of a past-life issue. For instance, many people I've worked with have received Divine guidance to become intuitive counselors or spiritual/alternative medicine healers. Yet, as much as they desire these goals, they feel an equal or greater amount of fear.

In many cases, these present-day healers had past lives where they were killed because of their intuitive or healing skills. I've worked with people who've had numerous lives of being beheaded, burned at the stake, or some other horrible form of death because their intuitive skills threatened local church or government institutions. They died in the Inquisition and during the witch-hunting eras. So, in this life, when they are Divinely guided to begin a counseling or a healing practice, is it any wonder that they feel profound fear? Actually, it's an intelligent decision if you think about it: "Let's see, I've been killed for being an intuitive before. I think I'll decide to *not* be openly intuitive in this life."

So, whether you believe in past lives or not, you can still benefit from the role that they play in applying Divine guidance to our *present* life. As I've said, Divine guidance has practical applications in helping us lead a happier, more harmonious life. However, many people unconsciously block the awareness of their Divine guidance. Or, they don't follow their guidance. The result is unanswered prayers—not because God and the angels are ignoring them, but because the Divine guidance is in limbo like a letter from heaven that the recipient refuses to open and read.

Here are some of the blocks related to past lives that prevent us from enjoying the benefits of applied Divine guidance:

**Past-life vows**—Ever get the feeling that you can't get ahead financially? Do your relationships seem chronically problem-ridden? Vows of poverty, celibacy, or suffering that you made in past lives may be the culprit. Again, regardless of whether you believe in past lives, it cannot hurt you—and it may just help—to sever vows that you may have made.

Here are some powerful affirmations to release the effects of such vows. I use this method with my clients who are blocked because of past-life interference, and the results are outstanding. The key to the efficacy of these affirmations hinges upon your saying them with conviction. In other words, you must *mean* what you are verbalizing instead of merely voicing the words. Say each of the following affirmations twice, either mentally or aloud, with great intent:

- *I hereby sever all vows of poverty I may have made in any lifetime, and I ask that all effects of those vows be undone in all directions of time.*

- *I hereby sever all vows of suffering I may have made in any lifetime, and I ask that all effects of those vows be undone in all directions of time.*

(**Note:** Do not say the following affirmation if you are currently following a purposely celibate lifestyle):

- *I hereby sever all vows of celibacy I may have made in any lifetime, and I ask that all effects of those vows be undone in all directions of time.*

**The fear of being powerful**—This particular fear often stems from past lives in which we *did* misuse our power. In particular, if we lived in the ancient civilization known as "Atlantis," the fear of misusing our power is prevalent.

Atlantis was a thriving society that used cutting-edge technology based upon crystal-driven and solar-powered energy. Atlanteans had many advanced methods for healing and transportation. Many of them also had an insatiable hunger for power. The Atlanteans used their technological know-how to develop weapons used for conquering other civilizations. One by one, Atlantis acquired power over many land masses in the world.

Ultimately, however, they misused their weaponry power and ended up destroying their own land mass. It sank in an explosion caused by weapons that were being deployed to overtake land on the other side of the world. To this day, souls who lived in Atlantis fear annihilating themselves and their loved ones through their abuse of power.

## Past-Life Issues, Present-Life Challenges

If you suspect, or know, that you had a traumatic past life that led you to close down your intuitive abilities, your angels can help you release this pain. Your angels can also help you heal any health challenges related to your past lives. I've worked with many clients and students who were born with injuries or other body issues that were directly related to the way they died in past lives.

For instance, a woman named Suzanne who was impaled by a sword during battle had chronic pain in her left hip—in the exact spot where she had received her past-life fatal injury. Another woman who was hanged in a past life suffered chronic neck pain in this life and was phobic about wearing tight-necked shirts. Both of these clients are among those who have successfully eradicated pain from their lives by inviting their angels to heal them.

It's not necessary to remember or recall your past life in order for your angels to heal you. However, sometimes the angels will let you know the association between present-life issues and unhealed pain from your past life. Almost always, the healing occurs when you release the pent-up emotions from your past life.

For instance, your angels may guide you to forgive those who killed you in a past life. They may help you release centuries-old feelings of horror that you've held in response to witnessing a wartime massacre. In those instances where it is helpful and therapeutic, your angels and your own unconscious mind will allow you to remember the past-life scenes. They will never show you any information for which you are emotionally unprepared.

My client Grace finally understood why she was so drawn to Celtic countries when she received an angel reading that helped her understand how her current self-esteem issues were tied to her past life:

**Grace**: Why do I feel so unworthy and inadequate, and what can I do about it?

**Doreen**: The angels tell me that you are healing from this, but it's going slower than you like. So, you are making progress with this issue. It's interesting. You have humility as one of your spiritual qualities and part of your purpose. Apparently, part of your life purpose was to come and learn about humility in this lifetime, because in a previous lifetime you did not have much humility at all.

Your angels show me a past life in which you were a privileged daughter of upper-class parents, and you were raised with a silver spoon. I have to be blunt about what they show me: You were really snotty and kind of looked down your nose at other people. But it was because you just didn't understand; that's all you knew. You had a wonderful life, and it wasn't a wasted life. But the way that you looked at people in general was colored by never having to go through any kind of challenges, and so you set up this life to balance that life and to learn humility.

But the trouble is that in many cases, you substituted humility for self-worth issues, when they are two separate things. And that's the lesson for you right now: How do you balance humility without going into shame or guilt? So the spiritual lesson, which is where you are headed on your learning path right now, is truly knowing the oneness of all of us. To know that the grandness of God is within each of us, including you. No one is more or less special than anyone else.

You still have that regalness from your past life with you. This looks like it was in a Celtic country, such as Wales or Ireland. You still have a little bit of standoffishness from that life, and that puts you into your ego state and makes you feel afraid. You're almost afraid of your natural reactions to other people, and so it's really about noticing and guarding your thoughts about other people.

As you see others, so you see yourself. If you can learn to see the bliss and beauty within others, then you'll more easily see it within yourself. Your angels say that you need to monitor your thoughts, and when you go into judgment about yourself or others, forgive yourself and let those thoughts go. Don't fight them or they'll increase in size and strength. Just notice the thoughts, and then let them go. But you're so close. Please let's not discount the progress that you've made! Your angels show me that you've just grown and grown in this issue. It's just learning to balance and not going to other extremes of self-judgment or other types of judgment. Both extremes always feel painful.

**Grace:** You're right, I have come a long way, and I need to give myself more credit for that.

**Doreen:** Well, we all have our moments of harshness about ourselves. The angels are here to help us heal this tendency because it really gets in our way more than it motivates us.

ॐ ॐ ॐ

Several of my clients have come to understand why they've had contentious relationships in this life. For example, a client named Bridgette realized that she'd had two problematic relationships in past lives with her mother. Those relationship issues had carried over into this life, where Bridgette and her mother constantly fought. Bridgette's angels helped her to realize that if she didn't heal her mother-daughter relationship in *this* life, she would probably have another lifetime battling with her mother in a *future* life. That was enough to motivate Bridgette to heal the relationship, with the help of her angels.

### Karma Releasing

*Karma* is a long-held belief system that says that everything we do is a "cause" of "effects" that we later experience. The belief in karma is one way of looking at the Universal law of cause and effect, but it is *not* the only way. Cause and effect is an untransmutable law, but this law does not hold that we should be "punished" or "blocked" because of our past experiences. On the contrary, the Law of Cause and Effect is a law of love, and it seeks to release us from our past.

For one thing, the idea of "past" is based on a belief in linear time. We know that time is actually simultaneous, not linear. In other words, everything you have ever experienced and *will* ever experience is happening now, right at this moment. That is because there *is* no other moment but now. Humans on Earth created the belief in past, present, and future time as a way of measuring their growth and accomplishments. However, the spiritual truth is that we all are already as accomplished as we could ever want to be. We're already home, perfect in all ways, since we are in union with God. The only "path" or "goal," if any, is to realize that we've already got everything we desire. As soon as we realize this fact, we experience it.

Let's put it another way, because it's very important that this concept be explained in clear and simple terms: There are several realities co-existing right now. A good analogy is to think of these realities as several movies that are each in a VCR on top of your television set. You can choose to watch any movie you like. You don't need permission from anyone else; you are the authority figure here. One movie is a really beautiful masterpiece, a magnificent film that inspires and empowers you. Another movie is a low-budget, mediocre film. Still another movie is a "comedy of errors," in which the characters get in and out of one jam after another. Then there's the tragedy, which is filled with heavy drama, heartaches, and problems of every imaginable type.

All of these movies co-exist simultaneously, each waiting to be played and experienced right now. Which movie will *you* play and experience? You decide based upon the thoughts that you choose to think. It's important for all of us to understand that we truly do choose our thoughts, and therefore, choose the movie—or type of life—that we experience. Everyone is equally qualified to choose and experience every movie. You don't have to earn your right to experience the beautiful, harmonious movie. A powerfully peaceful and meaningful life *is* your birthright. Although going through pain and obstacles is one way to achieve spiritual growth, it's not the only way. You truly can achieve enlightenment with a peaceful life, because you are already enlightened right now.

If you are experiencing lack, limitation, or pain of any kind, it simply means that somewhere within you, you are choosing thoughts of fear. Sometimes we're not even aware of these thoughts, or we believe that we have no control over them—as if the thoughts choose *us!* With practice, you can become aware of what type of thought is in your mind each moment. Whenever you feel pain of any kind, you'll know that you have held a fearful thought. As you progress on the spiritual path, you'll develop less tolerance for pain, until you reach a point of having a "zero tolerance for pain policy." At that point, you'll no longer hold fearful thoughts, and you'll instantly recognize and release any fearful thoughts that you may mistakenly choose on occasion. You can work with the angels in releasing the fearful thoughts and their effects. After all, the angels are always with you and always ready to help you. Just think, *Angels, please help me!* and they will intervene and heal.

Every loving thought and every fearful thought has an effect. Loving thoughts come from your true self. Fearful thoughts come from your false self, or ego.

Effects stay connected to their causes. Whenever you choose a fearful thought, it stays tethered to your ego-self, like a hot air balloon. Therefore, painful experiences stay connected to you—one after another, in a seemingly endless pattern and cycle—as long as you hang on to the *cause* or the ego's fearful thoughts. However, if you release the cause, its effect flies away along with it.

The beautiful bottom line of all of this is that all of the fearful thoughts that you have had, or that others may have had about you, can be released. Their painful effects can be released along with them!

In *A Course in Miracles*, it says, "Acknowledge but that you have been mistaken, and all effects of your mistakes will disappear." What the *Course* is saying is that we can "collapse time" by returning our thoughts to truth—the basis of true reality.

Nothing real can be threatened; nothing unreal exists. Herein lies the peace of God.

This is very different from shirking responsibility for your actions; and it is also very different from the religious concept of "atoning for sins." Releasing karma simply means releasing false ideas, which are causing painful effects. After all, mistakes don't require punishment, they simply require correction. All of us have made mistakes—some of us have made mistakes that we may consider practically "unforgivable." Yet, God sees right past those mistakes and instead sees our created perfection. We are powerful beings, but we're not powerful enough to undo the perfection that came with us being made in the image and likeness of our Creator. Nothing you could have ever said, thought, or done could have ever changed how perfectly wonderful you truly are and always will be.

In some of the afterlife astral planes, there is a belief that if you make mistakes in a lifetime—such as being cruel to another person—that you must reincarnate with some physical or emotional problems to "atone" for those mistakes. When you incarnate from this framework of thinking, you elect to have a lifetime of punishing pain and problems. However, you can escape from this mistake in thinking any time you choose.

The angels will help you release the effects of mistakes in thinking made in this lifetime or any lifetime. And it doesn't matter whether you believe in reincarnation or not.

### How the Angels Can Heal Past-Life Issues

Just by holding the intention to heal your past-life issues, your angels will be able to help you. In addition to having a formal session with a trained past-life regressionist, your angels can help you remember and release your past-life issues. You can accomplish this goal either in your sleep or during a meditative state:

**In your sleep**—Before you go to bed at night, mentally ask your angels to enter your dreams and show you any significant past lives that are related to your current-life issues. You will have dreams about other times in which you lived, and you may or may not remember these dreams, depending upon your unconscious mind's preparedness in handling the emotions.

It doesn't matter if you remember the dreams, from a healing standpoint. What matters is that, during these nighttime episodes, your angels have your permission to enter and heal your pent-up emotions. You should awaken feeling like you've done a lot of clearing-out work during your sleep. You may even feel a bit drained. Nonetheless, you'll know that you have engaged in important work in your sleep that will have a strong healing effect overall.

**In your meditations**—While in a meditative state, ask your angels to show you visions of your past lives. Then allow yourself to be focused, with an open mind. Don't strain to make anything happen. Instead, be like a passive movie screen that receives projections from the angels.

Your ego-mind may try to convince you that you're making up the pictures that you see in your mind's eye. Release these fears and concerns to your angels so that you don't interrupt the flow of information being sent to you.

As you watch or relive the past-life memories, be sure to maintain an awareness of your angels. Know that they were there with you in your past lives, and are with you now as you relive the old memories. Your angels will guide you so that you can heal and cleanse any past-life pain.

For example, they may ask you to imagine a different "ending" to your past-life movie, almost as if you are rewriting the script of that past life. So, instead of being traumatically killed, you invent a scene in which you die peacefully in your sleep. Your unconscious mind will override the old emotions with the new, more peaceful emotions.

Or, your angels may guide you to forgive yourself or other people in your past life. Be sure to ask your angels to help you accomplish this releasement, as you may find it difficult to forgive completely on your own. The angels will enter your cellular and emotional memory and clean away any residue of past-life negative emotions.

Here is a transcript of an angel therapy session with a client whose past-life issues were interfering with his present-life work and finances. Read how the angels helped him lift away his previous poverty patterns so that he could enjoy more prosperity and meaning in his profession:

**Sam**: I'm just getting ready to launch my own creatively based company. What do the angels say about this?

**Doreen**: You *must* do this type of work; the angels say you have no choice, because it is what and who you are.

**Sam**: Oh, yes, I definitely have a burning passion!

**Doreen**: Well, the angels show me that anything you do that involves artistic work will be enjoyable, and that there is a great potential for success. However, the angels say that you have some deservingness issues involving money. These beliefs of yours keep money one step ahead of you, instead of being in your possession in the current moment.

Your angels say that you are a very talented person, so talent is not the issue.

**Sam**: Oh okay, it's about knowing that I deserve to make money from my talents.

**Doreen**: Exactly! You've got this mental energy that keeps money from coming to you. The angels say you have an expectation that you won't have enough money.

**Sam**: Okay, I'm aware of that. I'm still aware that at some level I don't feel that I deserve money to come to me.

**Doreen**: The angels ask us to do some angel therapy on this issue right now, okay? Please take a very deep breath and see a beam of light going down through the center of your head, magnetizing any kind of stress or worries and eradicating them. I'd like to ask you to affirm with me, please: *I am willing to sever any vows of poverty that I may have made in any lifetime. I sever these vows of poverty now, and they are gone.*

**Sam**: I am willing to sever any vows of poverty that I may have made in any lifetime. I sever these vows of poverty now, and they are gone.

**Doreen**: Okay, great. There is just something in your subconscious mind that is seeing money a little differently than your angels would like you to see it. It's really important that you just see money as support for the beautiful work that you've been born to do, because you truly do intend to bring a lot of joy and merriment to the world through your work.

**Sam**: Well, that's exactly what I intend!

**Doreen**: You *have* to do this work. You have no choice because of this strong drive within you that comes from your Divine life mission. The only thing that you do have a choice about are your expectations of being supported while you do this work. That you deserve to *get* so that you can *give*.

**Sam**: Yes, that's definitely been an issue with me, particularly when I know that there are other people who are worse off than I. Also, in my upbringing, I've been given this message that, "poverty is holy." Even though for many years I've been intellectually aware that this message isn't true for me, it's been a difficult attitude to shake.

**Doreen**: Exactly. Well, in your prominent past life that relates to this one, you lived in England and you dressed like a court jester, but you didn't do that. Something similar, like a vaudeville act.

**Sam**: I've always been kind of drawn to the idea of the traveling minstrel.

**Doreen**: Exactly! That's what you were! A traveling minstrel, and what you did in that life is you "made do." You would stop in one community and do your work, and then you'd find some kind farmers and they'd take you in and board you for the night. And so that's the kind of lifestyle you had—a real carefree, "it's gonna come, I'll be taken care of" attitude. But it was almost like you were accepting the scraps of life on the other hand. In this life, we want you to take your standards up a notch.

**Sam**: Well, I feel ready to do that. Do you think that meditation is the answer?

**Doreen**: I think being conscious of this underlying attitude is the key for you. Your angels ask you to put your foot down to the universe and say, "Hey! I deserve to be fully supported for my work." Once you put your foot down to the universe, it really responds quickly.

**Sam**: Great! Well I'm at that point where I feel that I'm ready. I'm tired of doing artistic projects for big corporations, and I'm ready to follow my heart and create artwork from my soul. Do you feel that now is the right time for me to quit my regular commercial art job and go full-time into my own business?

**Doreen**: You should hang on to your regular job until you're really ready to do this other work, and you're ready to soar. In other words, when you have a firm knowingness that it's time. That knowingness won't come from fear or anger. It will come from a peaceful and quiet assurance that simply knows, "Now is the time." After all, you do have a wife, and you do have bills, and you're not a traveling minstrel in *this* life. If you were a single guy, I'd say, "Just go for it now."

As soon as you're mentally ready, you'll be able to make the break. So, you decide when that is. It's not written on any stones. Do it part-time to begin with.

**Sam**: I know on a deep level that my work will be successful. It's just a matter of me getting over the "pre-game jitters." I don't think it's going to take too much, though, for me to gain more confidence.

**Doreen**: You'll become more confident soon, I agree. Your angels and I would like to have you work with two archangels to help you further with your chosen career path. One is Archangel Gabriel, who is the angel of communicators and artists and people who serve through performing arts. Gabriel is a female archangel, and she can open up many doors for you. Even if you have no sense of her talking to you, you'll feel the evidence of her presence with opportunities.

The other archangel is Michael, who stands to your right at this moment. He's the protector angel, who is there to give you the courage to move forward.

**Sam:** That's interesting that the issue of courage comes up, because I feel that more than anything else right now, I need courage. I feel that Gabriel's energy has certainly been with me as an artistic communicator. But the courage to believe in myself and to know that it's okay to go out there and possibly make mistakes—I feel that this is my primary objective this year.

**Doreen:** Yes, absolutely. Since late 1998, we have all been experiencing a new energy that calls for us to live in complete integrity, and to let go of things that aren't honoring our true self. If we don't let go of them, we feel more and more pain. You really must do this work. Then, add on top of the mix this new energy of 1999, and you have to let go of this old stuff and move forward.

**Sam:** Yes, I definitely sense that strongly. On the last job I was working on, making a commercial brochure, I was feeling a heaviness that I hadn't felt on previous jobs. It was as if the heaviness was telling me, "It's time to move on." Yet I'm not feeling any anxiety that's pushing me forward. It's more of a peaceful strength.

ぐ ぐ ぐ

In the next chapter, you'll read about Earth angels who help us in surprising ways. You may discover that *you* are actually an Earth angel.

# CHAPTER ELEVEN

# Incarnated Angels, Elementals, Walk-Ins, and Star People

I'm often asked if angels ever incarnate in human form. The answer is most definitely yes. Hebrews 13:2 makes mention of this fact when it says, *"Be careful when entertaining strangers, for by so doing, many have entertained angels unawares."* In other words, you may have interacted with angels who look like humans without being aware that they actually were these heavenly beings. In fact, *you* may be an incarnated angel and not know it.

To me, an angel is anyone who acts angelically. In this respect, then, all of us are incarnated angels from time to time. People have come from all over the universe to live on Earth during this millennium shift. In my private psychic counseling practice, I've been able to get to know many people whose origins are not of this Earth. I've learned that there are many incarnated extraterrestrials (E.T.'s), angels, elementals, and walk-ins on the planet right now.

In the ultimate sense, we are all one—one with God, with each other, with the angels, and the ascended masters. Each of us has the same Divine spark of God-light within our core. Like multiple leaves attached to the same tree, we have the same source, and we affect each other.

However, in this illusory world where we appear to be separated beings, we do have outward characteristics that distinguish us from one another. For instance, those who are born male have an energy that is distinct from those who are born female.

There are also different wavelength energy patterns, depending on your lifestyle. Someone who, for example, spends most of his time drinking alcohol in a bar will have a different countenance and energy from someone who spends most of his time praying and meditating. Your energy pattern is affected by the places where you hang out, the people with whom you associate, and the thoughts that you predominantly think.

In the same way, there are souls who have "hung out" in most of their lives in different types of incarnations or locales. Not every child of God incarnates on Earth as a human. Some beings choose lives on other planets and other dimensions. If they have had several lives in these other places, their countenance and energy patterns reflect these surroundings and experiences. Then, when they do choose to come to Earth for an incarnation, they carry the energy patterns of their previous lives in these other places and dimensions.

Many "lightworkers" (people who are compelled to help others, especially in spiritual ways) have had previous incarnations in other dimensions or planets. They chose to incarnate in human form upon Earth at this time to act as Earth angels during the millennium shift.

In order to adjust to Earth life, they "borrowed" past-life memories from the Akashic Records (the afterlife plane library that contains records of everything that has ever happened to anyone). These borrowed past-life memories serve as buffers or cushions, so the soul will know what to expect on this planet. After all, Earth is considered one of the more volatile planets on which to incarnate. The level of aggression, violence, and pessimism here is considered quite high in the galaxies. A wonderful book on the topic of borrowed past-life memories is *Keepers of the Garden* by Dolores Cannon.

Not everyone who is an incarnated angel, star person, elemental, or walk-in is here for the first time. Those who act as Earth angels may choose to come here repeatedly. They retain the energy pattern of their realm of origination, so, for example, an incarnated angel has been in that form over her many lives.

### *Star People*

The first time I worked with an incarnated E.T.—whom I call a "star person," I was startled. She defied all of my stereotypes about extraterrestrials. She looked a lot like an ordinary person (although there are some subtle, but key physical distinctions among star people that I've listed below). Yet, until I psychically discerned that she was working with a spacecraft, I had no clue that she wasn't from Earth.

When I told my client that I was seeing her working and traveling on a large spacecraft, she readily agreed. She, unlike some of my subsequent star person clients, was very aware of her origins. Since working with this first star person, I've had the opportunity to work with a dozen more, and I found some interesting patterns among them:

- **Distinctive eyes**—Star people have eyes that are almond shaped or shaped like crescents, with the bars pointing down like on a letter *n*. Think of Bette Midler's eyes, and you've got the picture.

- **Petite frames**—Most incarnated star people have small bones, and they are thin and short in stature.

- **"Wallflower" looks**—They tend to have very plain facial features, and most of them dress very casually. It's as if they want to blend into the background and not call attention to themselves.

- **Unusual auras**—Star people have auras with stripes pointing away from the body, with the colorings of rainbows. Humans and beings from Earthly dimensions have auras that surround the body like an eggshell. These distinctive aura patterns show up on Kirlian and aura photographs.

- **Diffused life purposes**—Their life purposes are to "help as needed." Star people hold open doors for strangers and let people go ahead of them in long lines, without caring whether they get a thank you in response. They are here to be nice, to collectively diffuse the planet of stress and violence. Because of this diffused life purpose, star people don't usually have a specific life purpose, but instead, they've agreed to help whoever needs help. So, they frequently have ordinary jobs where they can reach a lot of people through their encouraging words and uplifting attitudes.

- **A love of peace and honesty**—They have very little tolerance for dishonesty and violence. They came from planets where these traits are nonexistent, so they do not know how to cope with humans who are inauthentic, manipulative, or violent. Because of this lack of coping skills with common Earth problems, incarnated E.T.'s are often mislabeled with psychiatric disorders, including attention deficit disorder (ADD) and schizophrenia.

- **Unusual relationships and family patterns**—Because their planets have different customs about family life, childbirth, reproduction, and sex, many star people don't contract to have Earthly marriages or children. They feel out-of-sync with Western culture's romantic images because this isn't their style. In addition, they know that family life would interfere with the lightwork that they contracted to do during their lifetime. Very often, a female star person will fall in love with a much younger man, who is a soulmate from their star group.

- **Feeling like they are different**—Star people know, deep down, that they aren't from Earth. They often spend their lives feeling like they don't fit in here. One star person said, "I've always had this sense that I was dropped off here on this planet, and I've been waiting for someone to return and take me home." They feel, deep down, that their biological family isn't their "true" family, and they wonder if they were adopted.

### *Incarnated Angels*

Another group of people whom I've gotten to know in my private practice are the incarnated angels. They, too, have distinguishing characteristics:

- **They look like angels**—Both male and female incarnated angels have sweet facial features, usually with heart-shaped faces and childlike features. A high percentage of female incarnated angels bleach or highlight their hair blonde.

- **Relationship challenges**—Incarnated angels have a history of co-dependent relationships due to their predisposition to giving, nurturing, and rescuing others. They also can see the best in everyone, so they often stay in abusive relationships longer than the average person would tolerate. Incarnated angels often have a history of multiple marriages and divorces.

- **Compulsive behaviors and weight issues**—Incarnated angels usually have histories of compulsive behaviors, especially overeating, and they are often overweight. They turn to food or other substances to deal with their emotional issues, especially if they are disconnected from their spirituality.

- **Professional helpers**—They are natural healers and helpers and often have healing or service work professions such as nursing, massage therapy, social work, the airline industry, or teaching. Strangers pour out their hearts to them, and they often say, "I don't know why I'm telling you such private things about myself. There's just something about you that I feel I can trust."

- **Givers, not receivers**—Incarnated angels are very generous people who sometimes have difficulty receiving. Consequently, they can manifest lack in their lives by blocking the flow of money, love, energy, and other natural resources from coming into their lives. Incarnated angels are very sensitive to others' feelings, often to the point of ignoring their own needs. This can lead these angels to feel frustrated or resentful when their own needs aren't met.

### *Incarnated Elementals*

The incarnated elementals are another group of "Earth angels" who are here to help. They are humans whose origination is the elemental kingdom, which consists of the leprechauns, fairies, brownies, and elves. Here are their distinguishing characteristics:

- **Celtic heritage or appearance**—They often have reddish hair, fair skin, and light eyes. Their ancestry is Irish or British.

- **They look like elementals**—Incarnated leprechauns *look* like the leprechauns depicted in children's books, both in their body appearance and in their facial features. The same holds true for incarnated elves and brownies. Incarnated fairies are usually slender and willowy females who are moderate to tall in height. It's rare to see an overweight or short incarnated fairy.

- **Characteristic clothing**—Incarnated elementals often dress in outfits that you might think would be characteristic of their particular elemental species. For instance, an incarnated leprechaun would dress in green outfits and prefer to wear comfortable shoes. Incarnated fairies opt for flowing, diaphanous gowns. And incarnated brownies often wear coarse, heavily woven outer garments, similar to that of a friar or monk.

- **Mischievous personalities**—They are prone to playing practical jokes, sometimes to the point of seeming passive-aggressive in their joking. It can be difficult to know if an incarnated elemental is kidding or being serious. Part of this personality aspect comes from the elemental's distrust or even dislike of humans.

- **An alignment with nature**—The elementals have a life purpose to protect Mother Earth and her animals from humans. So, elementals are best at careers that involve plants or animals, outdoor retreats; or ecological service work. They would be very happy doing volunteer work teaching humans, especially children, to respect animals and the planet. An incarnated elemental should never work in an office or anywhere where they are cooped up indoors. Most incarnated elementals relate to animals and plants better than they do to humans. As a result, many of them are reclusive or shy.

- **Manifesting skills**—Incarnated elementals are excellent at focusing their thoughts and quickly experiencing the results in reality. They can manifest massive wealth if they put their minds to it. However, incarnated elementals who focus on pessimism also can manifest problems and poverty very quickly, too.

## *Walk-Ins*

The fourth type of Earth angel is called a "walk-in." This is a being who incarnated through mutual agreement with a "walk-out," someone who left his or her being during an accident, illness, or while sleeping.

The walk-in is a highly evolved spiritual being with a lightworker life purpose. The walk-in needed to incarnate in a hurry for his or her purpose and decided to bypass the usual method of developing as a fetus, being born, and growing up. Instead, the walk-in soul located a living human who was not happy being alive. Perhaps the walk-in found a depressed or suicidal person, or a child who had difficulty adjusting.

The walk-in soul then communicated, usually through

dreams or thought-transfer, to the depressed person and said, "I will take over your responsibilities for you, and you will be able to go home to heaven without any negative repercussions associated with suicide." If the walk-out agreed to vacate his or her body and allow the walk-in full residency, then the two began to have trial swaps in which they tried out the arrangement several times.

If everything went smoothly, the walk-out then incurred a life-changing event such as a major illness or an accident. On occasion, the switch occurs when the walk-out is sleeping instead of during a crisis situation, but this is rare. At the agreed-upon time, the walk-out left his body, and the walk-in took up permanent residency.

Unlike a possession or attachment, the body only contains one soul, that of the walk-in. As everything is done with the full permission and cooperation of the walk-out, no negative or dark energies are involved.

The walk-in takes over the memory banks of the walk-out, and may not be aware that he or she is a walk-in. There are no set physical traits of a walk-in, since beings of all varieties become walk-ins and walk-outs. However, here are the distinguishing characteristics of a walk-in's life:

- **Drastic personality change**—Immediately after the walk-in occurred during an illness or accident, the person's friends and family members begin remarking, "You're so different—I almost feel like I don't know you anymore!"

- **Lifestyle change**—Newly incarnated walk-ins often find that they don't like the walk-out's lifestyle, so they make changes after coming into the body. They may divorce their spouse, quit their job, or move away. As part of the agreement with the walk-out, however, they take care of the previous person's responsibilities even during the transitions. So, lifestyle changes are handled as responsibly as possible.

- **Name change**—The walk-in may find that the previous person's name doesn't suit him or her. So, they may choose to change their first name, adopt a spiritual name, or change their full name.

### *If You Are an Earth Angel*

All four of the Earth angel groups are highly intuitive, yet they often have difficulty trusting their intuition. Partially, this comes from years of trying to adapt to Earth life. After all, the customs here are so foreign to their natural inclinations that star people and incarnated angels eventually learn to discount their inner feelings.

If you wonder whether you belong to any of these groups, then your inner guidance can tell you more. Before you go to sleep, say this affirmation to your higher self and spiritual group: *"Please give me a dream with clear messages about my origin that I will easily remember upon awakening."* You might also write this phrase on a piece of paper and place it under your pillow. When your subconscious is emotionally prepared, you will have a vivid lucid dream that will help you understand more about yourself.

Earth has many gifts to give to the world, including love, light, and lessons. My prayer is that, if you are among the above groups, you will open your heart and allow yourself to enjoy your time on this magnificent planet.

# CHAPTER TWELVE

# Number Sequences
from the Angels

The angels do their best to get our attention and to communicate with us. In this way, they help us heal our own lives. However, we often discount the signs that they give us, writing them off as mere coincidences or our imagination.

The angels say:

*"We can't write our messages to you in the sky.
You've got to pay attention and believe when you see
any patterns forming in your life—especially in
response to any questions or prayers that you've posed.
When you hear the same song repeatedly or see the
same number sequence, who do you think is behind
this? Your angels, of course!"*

## *Number Sequences*

Your angels often communicate messages to you by showing you sequences of numbers. They do this in two ways. First, they subtly whisper in your ear so that you'll look up in time to notice the clock's time or a phone number on a billboard. The angels hope you'll be aware that you're seeing this same number sequence repeatedly. For instance, you may frequently see the number sequence 111, and it seems that every time you look at a clock the time reads 1:11 or 11:11.

The second way in which the angels show you meaningful number sequences is by physically arranging for, say, a car to drive in front of you that has a specific license plate number they want you to see. Those who are aware of this phenomenon become adept at reading the meaning of various license plates. In this way, the angels will actually give you detailed messages (remember the Steve Martin character in the movie *L.A. Story,* where billboards kept giving him meaningful information?).

Here are the basic meanings of various number sequences. However, your own angels will tell you if your situation holds a different meaning for you. Ask your angels, "What are you trying to tell me?" and they'll happily give you additional information to help you decode their numeric meanings.

**111**—Monitor your thoughts carefully, and be sure to only think about what you want, not what you don't want. This sequence is a sign that there is a gate of opportunity opening up, and your thoughts are manifesting into form at record speeds. The 111 is like the bright light of a flashbulb. It means that the universe has just taken a snapshot of your thoughts and is manifesting them into form. Are you pleased with what thoughts the universe has captured? If not, correct your thoughts (ask your angels to help you with this if you have difficulty controlling or monitoring your thoughts).

222—Your newly planted ideas are beginning to grow into reality. Keep watering and nurturing them, and soon they will push through the soil so you can see evidence of your manifestation. In other words, don't quit five minutes before the miracle. Your manifestation is soon going to be evident to you, so keep up the good work! Keep holding positive thoughts, keep affirming, and continue visualizing.

333—The ascended masters are near you, desiring you to know that you have their help, love, and companionship. Call upon the ascended masters often, especially when you see the number 3 patterns around you. Some of the more famous ascended masters include Jesus, Moses, Mary, Quan Yin, and Yogananda.

444—The angels are surrounding you now, reassuring you of their love and help. Don't worry because the angels' help is nearby.

555—Buckle your seatbelts, because a major life change is upon you. This change should not be viewed as being "positive" or "negative," since all change is but a natural part of life's flow. Perhaps this change is an answer to your prayers, so continue seeing and feeling yourself being at peace.

666—Your thoughts are out of balance right now, focused too much on the material world. This number sequence asks you to balance your thoughts between heaven and earth. Like the famous "Sermon on the Mount," the angels ask you to focus on spirit and service, and know that your material and emotional needs will automatically be met as a result.

777—The angels applaud you—congratulations, you're on a roll! Keep up the good work and know that your wish is coming true. This is an extremely positive sign and means that you should also expect more miracles to occur.

**888**—A phase of your life is about to end, and this is a sign to give you forewarning so you can prepare. This number sequence may mean that you are winding up an emotional, career, or relationship phase. It also means that there is light at the end of the tunnel. In addition, it means, "The crops are ripe. Don't wait to pick and enjoy them." In other words, don't procrastinate making your move or enjoying the fruits of your labor.

**999**—Completion. This is the end of a big phase in your personal or global life. Also, it is a message to lightworkers involved in Earth healing and means, "Get to work because Mother Earth needs you right now."

**000**— A reminder that you are one with God, and to feel the presence of your Creator's love within you. Also, it is a sign that a situation has gone full circle.

### Number Combinations

The angels will often give you a message that involves a combination of two or more numbers. Here are the basic meanings of triple-digit, two-number combinations. If your messages contain three or more numbers, blend the answers from the different number combinations. For instance, if you continually notice the sequence 312, use the meaning of the 3 and 1 number combination, plus the 1 and 2 combination.

Or, if you feel guided, add the numbers together. Keep adding the subsequent digits together until you have a single-digit number. Then, look at the meaning for that particular number from the previously outlined list of number sequences that contain three identical numbers.

## Combinations of 1's

**1's and 2's, such as 121 or 112**—Our thoughts are like seeds that are beginning to sprout. You may have already seen some evidence of the fruition of your desires. These are signs that things will and are growing in your aspired direction. Keep the faith!

**1's and 3's, such as 133 or 113**—The ascended masters are working with you on your thought processes. In many ways, they are acting as mentors, teaching you the ancient wisdom involved in manifestation. They are sending you energy to keep you from feeling discouraged, and encouragement to stay focused on the true goals of your soul. Additionally, the ascended masters may be offering you advice, guidance, and suggestions on your life purpose. Always, however, they teach that every creation begins at the level of thought and idea. Ask them to help you choose wisely that which you want.

**1's and 4's, such as 114 or 144**—The angels are emphasizing strongly that you watch your thoughts right now. They counsel you to make a wish, as you are in a gateway that will manifest your thoughts right at this moment. (**Note:** 411 means "Ask the angels for some vital information that you need right now.")

**1's and 5's, such as 115, or 551**—Your thoughts are creating the changes in your life. Keep steering your thoughts in your desired direction. If the changes that you see forthcoming are not desired, you can stop or alter them by modifying your thoughts.

**1's and 6's, such as 116 or 661**—Keep your thoughts heavenward, and let go of materially minded worries. (**Note:** 611 means "Ask for help in repairing something in the material world that is irritating or bothering you right now.")

**1's and 7's, such as 117 or 771**—This is confirmation that you are doing great. You are on the right path, so keep going! This is a sign that you have chosen your thoughts well and that you should focus even more steadily on your objectives. Be sure to add appropriate emotions to your thoughts; for instance, feeling grateful for the gifts you have in life. Gratitude will speed the process of your manifestations.

**1's and 8's, such as 181 or 818**—You are nearing the end of a significant phase of your life. If you are tired of some part of your life, be glad that it will soon be healed or replaced with something better. Surrender and release those parts of your life that aren't working, as your thoughts of a better life are coming to pass.

**1's and 9's, such as 119 or 199**—A new door has opened for you as a product of your thoughts. You now have the opportunity to stare your thoughts in the face and come eye-to-eye with your own creations. Let the old fall away, as it is replaced with the new in accordance with your desires.

**1's and 0's, such as 100 or 110**—Powerful Divine guidance from God and the angels asks you to alter your thoughts. Perhaps you have been praying to be happier and healthier. If so, this is an answer to your prayers. God knows that the solution you seek is born within your thoughts. Ask God to guide the direction of your thoughts and support you during your time of transition.

## Combinations of 2's

**2's and 1's, such as 221 or 112**—Your thoughts are like seeds that are beginning to sprout. You may have already seen some evidence of the fruition of your desires. These are signs that things will and are growing in your aspired direction. Keep the faith!

**2's and 3's, such as 223 or 323**—The ascended masters are working with you as co-creators of your new project. They are telling you that they share your excitement and know that everything is working out well for you. The masters can see that your future is already guaranteed to be filled with the happiness you seek. Enjoy this new phase of your life!

**2's and 4's, such as 224 or 244**—As it says in the spiritual text, *A Course in Miracles*, "The angels nurse your newborn purpose." This is a sign that you have help from above in making your desired transitions. This is a time when you especially need to know that you're not alone. The 2 and 4 number sequences are a signal from your angels to tell you that they're working very closely with you right now.

**2's and 5's, such as 255 or 225**—Your prayers and intentions have been clear, strong, and without reservations; therefore, expect a change to come about faster than you may have foreseen. Don't let it throw you when your wishes come true. They may come about in unexpected ways, so hold on to your faith. Talk to God often, and ask for reassurance.

**2's and 6's, such as 266 or 226**— A new purchase or acquisition is coming your way.

**2's and 7's, such as 277 or 272**—Have you recently applied for a new job, admission to a school, or a loan? These numbers signal good news. They ask you to hang tight and to not allow your faith to waver.

**2's and 8's, such as 288 or 282**—One door is beginning to open, and another door is beginning to close. Be sure to listen to your intuition very closely right now, as it will guide you to take steps that will ensure your steady abundance during these transitions.

**2's and 9's, such as 299 or 292**—If you've recently suffered a loss (job, lover, etc.), expect it to be replaced in the very near future. Everything is working in your favor, although there may be so much behind-the-scenes activity involved that you wonder if God has forgotten about you. Worry not! Feel the energy of your life, which *is* moving forward right now. You are not being punished by your recent loss. The universe is, instead, preparing you for newness.

**2's and 0's, such as 200 or 202**—God wants you to know that He has not forgotten or abandoned you. He loves you very, very much! In fact, God is orchestrating a wonderful new phase of your life. Talk to God often, and you'll feel this forthcoming miracle. God also reminds you of the importance of "Divine timing." Sometimes, certain factors need to fall into place *first* before your desired outcome can be reached. As long as you hold strong in your thoughts and faith, there is nothing blocking you from attaining your desire.

## Combinations of 3's

**3's and 1's, such as 311 or 313**—The ascended masters are working with you on your thought processes. In many ways, they are acting as mentors, teaching you the ancient wisdom involved in manifestation. They are sending you energy to keep you from feeling discouraged, and encouragement to stay focused on the true goals of your soul. Additionally, the ascended masters may be offering you advice, guidance, and suggestions on your life purpose. Always, however, they teach that every creation begins at the level of thought and idea. Ask them to help you choose wisely that which you want.

**3's and 2's, such as 322 or 332**—The ascended masters are working with you as co-creators of your new project. They are telling you that they share your excitement and know that everything is working out well for you. The masters can see that your future is already guaranteed to be filled with the happiness you seek. Enjoy this new phase of your life!

**3's and 4's, such as 334 or 344**—You have *a lot* of help around you right now! Both the ascended masters *and* the angels are here to assist, guide, and love you. Reach out to them, as they are reaching out to you.

**3's and 5's, such as 353 or 335**—The ascended masters want to prepare you for a big life change that is imminent. They want you to know that they are holding your hand through this change and that everything will be all right. Embrace the change, and look for the blessings within it.

**3's and 6's, such as 363 or 336**—Your ascended masters are helping you manifest the material items you need for your Divine life purpose. Whether that means money for tuition or outlets for you to conduct your teaching or healing work, the masters are working to bring it to you. They want you to know that you deserve to receive this help, as it will better enable you to give to others.

**3's and 7's, such as 377 or 373**—The ascended masters are joyful. Not only do they see your true inner Divinity, but they also agree with the path that you have chosen. They want you to know that you deserve happiness, and to allow the flow of holy bliss that comes with your Divine heritage and chosen path.

**3's and 8's, such as 338 or 383**—"Keep going," the masters say to you. Boost the energy and focus of your thoughts and feelings. Realign your outlook with the knowledge of your oneness with God, everyone, and all of life.

**3's and 9's, such as 393 or 339**—This is a strong message to let go of situations in your life that aren't in integrity or that have served their purpose. Do not artificially hang on to situations because of fear. Know that each and every moment you are taken care of. It is vital that you hold a positive viewpoint about yourself and your future. This viewpoint actually *creates* what you will experience, so ask the masters to help you choose your thoughts from the high point of love.

**3's and 0's, such as 300 or 330**—God and the ascended masters are trying to get your attention, most likely with respect to a matter related to your Divine life purpose. Is there any guidance that you've been ignoring lately? If so, you may be feeling stuck right now. This number sequence is heaven's way of alerting you to the fact that you must do your part in the co-creation process. This means listening to and following your Divine guidance to take certain actions.

### Combinations of 4's

**4's and 1's, such as 441 or 411**—The angels are recommending that you watch your thoughts right now. They counsel you to make a wish, as you are in a gateway that will manifest your thoughts right at this moment. (**Note:** 411 means "Ask the angels for some vital information that you need right now.")

**4's and 2's, such as 422 or 442**—As it says in the spiritual text *A Course in Miracles*, "The angels nurse your newborn purpose." This is a sign that you have help from above in making your desired transitions. This is a time when you especially need to know that you're not alone. The 2 and 4 number sequences are a signal from your angels to tell you that they're working very closely with you right now.

**4's and 3's, such as 443 or 433**—You have *a lot* of help around you right now! Both the ascended masters *and* the angels are here to assist, guide, and love you. Reach out to them, as they are reaching out to you.

**4's and 5's, such as 455 or 445**—Your angels are involved in one of your significant life changes right now.

**4's and 6's, such as 446 or 466**—Your angels caution you that your focus is too much on the material world. They ask you to surrender your worries to them so that they can intervene. Balance your focus between heaven and earth, and know that your supply is truly unlimited, especially when you work hand-in-hand with the Divine.

**4's and 7's, such as 477 or 447**—The angels congratulate you and say, *"Keep up the great work! You are on a roll. Keep your thoughts focused, because it's having a big and positive effect."*

**4's and 8's, such as 488 or 448**—This is a message from your angels that a phase of your life is about to end. They want you to know that as things slow down, they are with you and will be helping to guide you to a new situation better suited to your needs, desires, and purpose.

**4's and 9's, such as 494 or 449**—The angels say to you that it's time to let go of a situation that has ended. They remind you that, as one door closes, another one opens. The angels are certainly helping you to open new doors and to heal from any pain that accompanies the transition that you are now undergoing. Please ask your angels to help you have faith that these endings and beginnings are answers to your prayers.

**4's and 0's, such as 440 or 400**—God and the angels want you to know that you are very, very loved. They ask you to take a moment to feel this love, as it will answer many of your questions and resolve any challenge.

## Combinations of 5's

**5's and 1's, such as 511 or 515**—Your thoughts are creating the changes in your life. Keep steering your thoughts in your desired direction. If the changes that you see forthcoming are not desired, you can stop or alter them by modifying your thoughts.

**5's and 2's, such as 522 or 552**—Your prayers and intentions have been clear, strong, and without reservations. Therefore, expect a change to come about faster than you may have foreseen. Don't let it throw you when your wishes come true. They may come about in unexpected ways, so hold on to your faith. Talk to God often, and ask for reassurance.

**5's and 3's, such as 533 or 553**—The ascended masters want to prepare you for a big life change that is imminent. They want you to know that they are holding your hand through this change and that everything will be all right. Embrace the change, and look for the blessings within it.

**5's and 4's, such as 554 or 544**—Your angels are involved in one of your significant life changes right now.

**5's and 6's, such as 556 or 566**—Your material life is changing significantly, such as a new home, car, or other possession.

**5's and 7's, such as 577 or 575**—This is a validation that you are "on target" with an impending change that will enrich you either physically, emotionally, or intellectually—or a combination of all three. Stay on course and you will soon see the evidence of how the changes add to your own life and to that of those around you.

**5's and 8's, such as 588 or 558**—This number sequence signifies that you are at the 11th hour, right before the change. Do not fear it, as you will be supported and loved throughout this change, which is now imminent.

**5's and 9's, such as 599 or 595**—In order for the new change to manifest, it's important to release the past. This number sequence asks you to let go of the old and know that it served a vital function during its time. However, life is fluid and change is inevitable. Know that the new is standing at your doorway, waiting for you to let it in. You invite the new in as you detach with love from the old.

**5's and 0's, such as 500 or 550**—An important message that lets you know that your life changes are in Divine and perfect order. They are a gift from God and in alignment with God's will for your higher self.

## Combinations of 6's

**6's and 1's, such as 611 or 661**—Keep your thoughts heavenward, and let go of materially minded worries. (**Note:** 611 means "Ask for help in repairing something in the material world that is irritating or bothering you right now.")

**6's and 2's, such as 622 or 662**—A new purchase or acquisition is coming your way.

**6's and 3's, such as 663 or 633**—Your ascended masters are helping you manifest the material items you need for your Divine life purpose. Whether that means money for tuition, or outlets for you to conduct your teaching or healing work, the masters are working to bring it to you. They want you to know that you deserve to receive this help, as it will better enable you to give to others.

**6's and 4's, such as 644 or 664**—Your angels caution you that your focus is too much on the material world. They ask you to surrender your worries to them so that they can intervene. Balance your focus between heaven and earth, and know that your supply is truly unlimited, especially when you work hand-in-hand with the Divine.

**6's and 5's, such as 665 or 655**—Your material life is changing significantly, such as a new home, car, or other possession.

**6's and 7's, such as 667 or 677**—A validation that your thoughts and work with the material world are right on the mark. You have successfully balanced your thoughts and activities so that you are taking care of the mind, body, and spirit. Keep up the great work!

**6's and 8's, such as 668 or 688**—You are about to part ways with something in your material world, such as selling a possession. If you do not intend to lose or sell anything in your material life, you can change your thoughts and alter this direction. However, if you are intent on selling or detaching from something material in your life, consider this a sign that your wish is about to come true.

**6's and 9's, such as 669 or 699**—Detach from your material items, especially if you have had any obsession with any particular type of material possession. This number sequence asks you to let go and detach. Also, this is a message that something in your life that you have sold or lost is about to be replaced with something better. Be open to receiving new possessions that exceed your expectations, as you are ready to be upgraded. You deserve the best!

**6's and 0's, such as 600 or 660**—This is a message from your Creator about your material life. Divine guidance from God asks you to focus less on Earthly desires. It's not that God is asking you to live an impoverished life, but rather, that your Creator asks you to try a more spiritual approach to having your needs met. Know that God is within you and is your source for everything you need. Simply hold faith and gratitude, and be open to signs or new opportunities that will bring your material needs to you. *"Seek ye first the kingdom of God, and all the rest will be added unto you"* is the heart of this number sequence's message. You can get more information on this process by reading *The Abundance Book* by John Randolph Price (published by Hay House) or by reading "The Sermon on the Mount" in the Gospel of Matthew.

## Combinations of 7's

**7's and 1's, such as 711 or 771**—This is confirmation that you are doing great. You are on the right path, so keep going! This is a sign that you have chosen your thoughts well, and it should inspire you to focus even more steadily on your objectives. Be sure to add appropriate emotions to your thoughts—for instance, feeling grateful for the gifts you have in life. Gratitude will speed the process of your manifestations.

**7's and 2's, such as 722 or 772**—Have you recently applied for a new job, admission to a school, or a loan? These numbers signal good news. They ask you to hang tight and not to allow your faith to waver.

**7's and 3's, such as 773 or 733**—The ascended masters are joyful. Not only do they see your true inner Divinity, but they also agree with the path that you have chosen. They want you to know that you deserve happiness, and to allow the flow of holy bliss that comes with your Divine heritage and chosen path.

**7's and 4's, such as 774 or 774**—The angels congratulate you and say, *"Keep up the great work! You are on a roll. Keep your thoughts focused, because it's having a big and positive effect."*

**7's and 5's, such as 775 or 755**—This is a validation that you are "on target" with an impending change that will enrich you either physically, emotionally, or intellectually—or a combination of all three. Stay on course and you will soon see the evidence of how the changes add to your own life, and to that of those around you.

**7's and 6's, such as 776 or 766**—A validation that your thoughts and work with the material world are right on the mark. You have successfully balanced your thoughts and activities so that you are taking care of the mind, body, and spirit. Keep up the great work!

**7's and 8's, such as 778 or 788**—Have you been feeling that some part of your life, such as a job or a relationship, is ending? This is a validation that your feelings are correct. The end could mean a significant positive change in the situation, or it could mean that some part of your life is nearing completion. Regardless, this number sequence heralds good news about a forthcoming positive change involving the completion of an intense situation. Hang tight, because your life is about to get easier.

**7's and 9's, such as 779 or 799**—Congratulations! You are shedding old parts of your life that no longer fit who you are. You are living a more authentic life that is in integrity with your highest view of yourself. This number sequence applauds your decisions to live honestly.

**7's and 0's, such as 700 or 770**—An "atta boy" or "atta girl" directly from God, giving you accolades for the mental, spiritual, and physical work you've been doing. You are helping yourself and many other people with your current path, and God asks you to continue with your great work.

## Combinations of 8's

**8's and 1's, such as 811 or 881**—You are nearing the end of a significant phase of your life. If you are tired of some part of your life, be glad that it will soon be healed or replaced with something better. Surrender and release those parts of your life that aren't working, as your thoughts of a better life are coming to pass.

**8's and 2's, such as 822 or 882**—One door is beginning to open, and another door is beginning to close. Be sure to listen to your intuition very closely right now, as it will guide you to take steps that will ensure your steady abundance during these transitions.

**8's and 3's, such as 883 or 833**—*"Keep going,"* the masters say to you. Boost the energy and focus of your thoughts and feelings. Realign your outlook with the knowledge of your oneness with God, everyone, and all of life.

**8's and 4's, such as 884 or 844**—This is a message from your angels that a phase of your life is about to end. They want you to know that as things slow down, they are with you and will be helping to guide you to a new situation better suited to your needs, desires, and purpose.

**8's and 5's, such as 885 or 855**—This number sequence signifies that you are at the 11th hour, right before the change. Do not fear this change, as you will be supported and loved throughout this change, which is now imminent.

**8's and 6's, such as 886 or 866**—You are about to part ways with something in your material world, such as selling a possession. If you do not intend to lose or sell anything in your material life, you can change your thoughts and alter this direction. However, if you are intent on selling or detaching from something material in your life, consider this a sign that your wish is about to come true.

**8's and 7's, such as 887 or 877**—Have you been feeling that some part of your life, such as a job or a relationship, is ending? This is a validation that your feelings are correct. The end could mean a significant positive change in the situation, or it could mean that some part of your life is nearing completion. Regardless, this number sequence heralds good news about a forthcoming positive change involving the completion of an intense situation. Hang tight, because your life is about to get easier.

**8's and 9's, such as 889 or 899**—Some significant phase in your life has come to an end, bringing with it other events that will also end in a domino effect. Like a train coming to the end of the line, one car will stop while the following train cars will take a moment to slow down before stopping. This number sequence is a message that you are going through a chain of event, where many parts of your life are slowing and stopping. Worry not, though, because these changes are necessary for new sequences and circumstances to begin for you.

**8's and 0's, such as 800 or 808**—A message from your Divine Creator, signifying that the impending endings are part of your overall Divine plan. They are answers to your prayers, and are in alignment with God's will for you. Ask God to help you allay any fears or worries you may have about these upcoming changes.

## Combinations of 9's

**9's and 1's, such as 991 or 919**—A new door has opened for you as a product of your thoughts. You now have the opportunity to stare your thoughts in the face and come eye-to-eye with your own creations. Let the old fall away, as it is replaced with the new in accordance with your desires.

**9's and 2's, such as 992 or 922**—If you've recently suffered a loss (job, lover, etc.), expect it to be replaced in the very near future. Everything is working in your favor, although there may be so much behind-the-scenes" activity involved that you wonder if God has forgotten about you. Worry not! Feel the energy of your life, which *is* moving forward right now. You are not being punished by your recent loss. The universe is, instead, preparing you for newness.

**9's and 3's, such as 993 or 939**—A strong message to let go of situations in your life that aren't in integrity or that have served their purpose. Do not artificially hang on to situations because of fears. Know that each and every moment you are taken care of. It is vital that you hold a positive viewpoint about yourself and your future. This viewpoint actually *creates* what you will experience, so ask the masters to help you choose your thoughts from the high point of love.

**9's and 4's, such as 994 or 944**—The angels say to you that it's time to let go of a situation that has ended. They remind you that as one door closes, another one opens. The angels are certainly helping you open new doors and to heal from any pain that accompanies the transition that you are now undergoing. Please ask your angels to help you to have faith that these endings and beginnings are answers to your prayers.

**9's and 5's, such as 959 or 995**—In order for the new change to manifest, it's important to release the past. This number sequence asks you to let go of the old and know that it served a vital function during its time. However, life is fluid and change is inevitable. Know that the new is standing at your doorway, waiting for you to let it in. You invite the new in as you detach with love from the old.

**9's and 6's, such as 966 or 996**—Detach from your material items, especially if you have had any obsession with any particular type of material possession. This number sequence asks you to let go and detach. Also, it is a message that something in your life that you have sold or lost is about to be replaced with something better. Be open to receiving new possessions that exceed your expectations, as you are ready to be upgraded. You deserve the best!

**9's and 7's, such as 977 or 997**—Congratulations! You are shedding old parts of your life that no longer fit who you are. You are living a more authentic life that is in integrity with your highest view of yourself. This number sequence applauds your decisions to live honestly.

**9's and 8's, such as 998 or 988**—Some significant phase in your life has come to an end, bringing with it other events that will also end in a domino effect. Like a train coming to the end of the line, one car will stop while the following train cars will take a moment to slow down before stopping. This number sequence is a message that you are going through a chain of events where a lot of parts of your life are slowing and stopping. Worry not, though, because these changes are necessary for new sequences and circumstances to begin for you.

**9's and 0's, such as 900 or 909**—This is a message from your Creator signifying that the part of your life that has just ended is Divinely guided. Nothing is ever truly lost. There is no death, and there are no accidents. Your recent life change, in which a significant part of your life has been halted or altered, is actually an answer to your prayer. God is letting you know that He is not taking anything away from you or "causing" your loss. Rather, your life plan or prayers called this life change to you, through your own God-given power. Be willing to forgive everyone involved so that you can be light and free as you enter into a beautiful new phase of life.

## Combinations of 0's

**0's and 1's, such as 001 or 010**—Powerful Divine guidance from God and the angels asks you to alter your thoughts. Perhaps you have been praying to be happier and healthier. If so, this is an answer to your prayers. God knows that the solution for which you seek is born within your thoughts. Ask God to guide the direction of your thoughts, and support you during your time of transition.

**0's and 2's, such as 002 or 020**—God wants you to know that He has not forgotten or abandoned you. He loves you very, very much! In fact, God is orchestrating a wonderful new phase of your life for you. Talk to God often, and you'll feel this forthcoming miracle. God also reminds you about the importance of "Divine timing." Sometimes certain factors need to fall into place *first* before your desired outcome can be reached. As long as you hold strong in your thoughts and faith, there is nothing blocking you from attaining your desire.

**0's and 3's, such as 003 or 300**—God and the ascended masters are trying to get your attention, most likely related to your Divine life purpose. Is there any guidance that you've been ignoring lately? If so, you may be feeling stuck right now. This number sequence is heaven's way of alerting you to the fact that you must do your part in the co-creation process. This means listening to and following your Divine guidance to take certain actions.

**0's and 4's, such as 040 or 400**—God and the angels want you to know that you are very, very loved. They ask you to take a moment to feel this love, as it will answer many of your questions and resolve any challenge.

**0's and 5's, such as 050 or 500**—An important message that lets you know that your life changes are in Divine and perfect order. They are a gift from God, and in alignment with God's will for your higher self.

**0's and 6's, such as 006 or 066**—A message from your Creator about your material life. Divine guidance from God asks you to let go of being overly focused on Earthly desires. It's not that God is asking you to live an impoverished life, but that your Creator asks you to have a more spiritual approach to having your needs met. Know that God is within you and is your source for everything you need. Simply hold faith and gratitude, and be open to intuition or new opportunities that will bring your material needs to you. *"Seek ye first the kingdom of God, and all the rest will be added unto you"* is the heart of this number sequence's message. You can get more information on this process by reading *The Abundance Book* by John Randolph Price (published by Hay House) or by reading "The Sermon on the Mount" in the Gospel of Matthew.

**0's and 7's, such as 007 or 070**—A pat on the back from God, giving you accolades for the mental, spiritual, and physical work you've been doing. You are helping yourself and many other people with your current path, and God asks you to continue with your great work.

**0's and 8's, such as 088 or 080**—A message from your Divine Creator signifying that the impending endings are part of your overall Divine plan. They are answers to your prayers, and are in alignment with God's will for you. Ask God to help you allay any fears or worries you may have about these upcoming changes.

**0's and 9's, such as 099 or 090**—A message from your Creator signifying that the part of your life that has just ended is Divinely guided. Nothing is ever truly lost. There is no death and there are no accidents. Your recent life change, in which a significant part of your life has been halted or altered, is actually an answer to your prayer. God is letting you know that He is not taking anything away from you or "causing" your loss. Rather, your life plan or prayers called this life change to you through your own God-given power. Be willing to forgive everyone involved so that you can be light and free as you enter into a beautiful new phase of life.

# APPENDIX

# "Forgiveness, Free Yourself Now" Exercise

Anyone can feel more at peace and more energized through the process of forgiveness. This process reminds me of throwing off weights when riding in a hot air balloon so you can go higher up. Old anger, fear, and resentment are dead weights that slow us and drain our vitality. Perhaps you have some weight you can throw over the side of your hot air balloon right now. When you forgive the world—including yourself—you become lighter and much less fearful.

This process takes between 30 and 60 minutes to complete, and believe me, it is a worthwhile time investment. Many clients report that this single exercise immediately transforms their lives in powerfully positive ways. Here are some steps to freedom through forgiveness:

1. **Know the benefits of forgiveness**—Forgiveness is different from saying, "I lose," or "I was wrong, and you were right." It is different from letting someone off the hook for a perceived wrong deed. Forgiveness is simply a way of freeing your spirit and becoming an unlimited being. Peacefulness and increased energy are the prizes, and forgiveness is the price. To me, it's a bargain.

2. **Take a forgiveness inventory**—(This exercise is partially based on the work of author John Randolph Price.) Write the name of *every* person, living or deceased, who has ever irritated you. Most people find they have a three- or four-page list and are able suddenly to remember names of people they hadn't thought about in years. Some people put down names of pets who irritated them, and almost everyone writes their own name somewhere on the list.

3.  **Release and forgive**—In a solitary room where no interruptions are possible, go down the list one name at a time. Hold the image of each person in your mind and tell him or her, "I forgive you and I release you. I hold no unforgiveness back. My forgiveness for you is total. I am free and you are free." This process may take 30 minutes or longer. However, it's important to stick with it until the entire list is complete.

4.  **Do nightly releasements**—Every evening before retiring, do a mental review of the day. Is there anyone you need to forgive? Just as you probably wash your face every night, it's also important to cleanse your consciousness nightly so resentment won't accumulate.

# The Corral Visualization

After relaxing with several slow, deep breaths, close your eyes and get into a comfortable position.

*Imagine that you are standing in a country field. A road is leading to you—one that brings all your material, emotional, and spiritual supplies. The road passes through a corral to get to you. The corral has two gates: one facing the road, and one facing you. If both gates are open, supplies readily flow to you, and your gifts to the world flow from you.*

*Whenever we hold unforgiveness toward someone, we imprison that person in our minds where we mentally flog them with our pronouncements of guilt and blame. The image of the person we resent is "corralled" in our consciousness, and the gates to the corral slam shut like prison doors. You necessarily go into the corral along with the person you've judged in order to monitor their imprisonment. So, both gates are shut, and your locked corral blocks your flow and supply.*

*Look inside your corral right now and see who's there. See the high price you pay for corralling these people. If you are ready to forgive, imagine the gates of your corral automatically opening. Visualize whoever is in the corral walking out, free, happy, and forgiven. Wish them well. If this seems difficult, try forgiving the person instead of their deeds. As you forgive, feel the release, the relief, and the renewed energy as your resentment lifts. Check to make sure that you're not in the corral alone out of an ego judgment you hold against yourself.*

Recheck your corral often, especially when you feel tired, ill, or afraid. You'll find that these are the times when you have the most people (including yourself) locked into your corral. Once you open the gates and clear the corral, your emotions and energy level will improve.

# Angel Affirmations

Say these affirmations daily to increase your self-confidence and self-love. You can record them in your own voice, which will give you a powerful affirmations tape, or photocopy this page and post them in a prominent place. Add your own personal affirmations related to your goals and desires.

- *I am now surrounded by angels.*
- *The angels shine the love of God upon me and through me.*
- *I accept this love from God and the angels.*
- *I deserve love.*
- *I deserve happiness.*
- *I deserve health.*
- *I deserve help from heaven, and I accept it now.*
- *I call upon God and the angels to help and guide me.*
- *I listen to my inner voice and feelings.*
- *My inner voice and feelings is guidance from God and the angels.*
- *This guidance is everything I need.*
- *I follow my guidance in full faith.*
- *I know that God and the angels love me and are guiding me right now.*
- *I accept the angels' love.*
- *I accept love.*
- *I love.*
- *I am love.*
- *I am loving.*

- *I am very loved.*
- *Everyone loves me.*
- *I love everyone.*
- *I forgive everyone.*
- *I forgive myself.*
- *I send God's love to everyone I meet.*
- *I guard my thoughts carefully and only allow positive and loving thoughts to come through.*
- *There is an abundance of love in the world.*
- *There is enough for everyone.*
- *There is plenty to go around.*
- *I have an abundance of everything.*
- *I attract wonderful, loving people into my life.*
- *My angels and I enjoy new opportunities to give service to the world.*
- *I am rewarded constantly.*
- *My life is harmonious and peaceful.*
- *I am peaceful.*
- *I am radiant.*
- *I am joyful.*

# About the Author

**Doreen Virtue** (yes, that *is* her real name) is a spiritual doctor of psychology and the author of numerous books, including *Divine Guidance, Angel Therapy, The Lightworker's Way,* and the audio programs *Healing with the Angels* and *Chakra Clearing.*

Dr. Virtue gives workshops on spiritual psychological issues across North America, discussing angel therapy, angel communication, and spiritual healing. Many of her students are medical and psychological professionals, including M.D.'s, R.N.'s, psychologists, and social workers. Doreen's clairvoyance allows her to see and communicate with angels of people who are physically with her, as well as people whom she talks to over the telephone. Consequently, the media frequently ask Doreen to give "angel readings" on the air and via telephone, in which she describes and converses with audience members' guardian angels and deceased loved ones. Dr. Virtue has appeared on *Oprah,* CNN, *Good Morning America, The View* with Barbara Walters, and other programs. Her work has been featured in *Redbook, Woman's Day, USA Today,* and national and regional publications.

For information on Dr. Virtue's workshops, please contact Hay House or visit her Website at **www.AngelTherapy.com**.

# Hay House Titles
## of Related Interest

**YOU CAN HEAL YOUR LIFE,** *the movie,*
starring Louise L. Hay & Friends
(available as a 1-DVD program and an expanded 2-DVD set)
Watch the trailer at: **www.LouiseHayMovie.com**

**THE SHIFT,** *the movie,*
starring Dr. Wayne W. Dyer
(available as a 1-DVD prog-ram and an expanded 2-DVD set)
Watch the trailer at: **www.DyerMovie.com**

### Books

***Adventures of a Psychic:*** *The Fascinating and Inspiring*
*True-Life Story of One of America's Most Successful Clairvoyants,*
by Sylvia Browne

***Big George:*** *The Autobiography of an Angel*

***Born to Be Together:*** *Love Relationships, Astrology,*
*and the Soul,* by Terry Lamb

***Developing Your Intuition with Magic Mirrors***
(book and card pack), by Uma Reed

***The Experience of God:*** *How 40 Well-Known Seekers*
*Encounter the Sacred,* by Jonathan Robinson

***The Indigo Children:*** *The New Kids Have Arrived,*
by Lee Carroll and Jan Tober

***Prayer and the Five Stages of Healing,***
by Ron Roth, Ph.D., with Peter Occhiogrosso

ॐ ॐ ॐ

All of the above are available at your local bookstore,
or may be ordered by visiting Hay House (see next page).

We hope you enjoyed this Hay House book. If you'd like to receive our online catalog featuring additional information on Hay House books and products, or if you'd like to find out more about the Hay Foundation, please contact:

Hay House, Inc.
P.O. Box 5100
Carlsbad, CA 92018-5100

**(760) 431-7695 or (800) 654-5126**
**(760) 431-6948 (fax) or (800) 650-5115 (fax)**
**www.hayhouse.com® • www.hayfoundation.org**

༄ ༄ ༄

*Published and distributed in Australia by:*
Hay House Australia Pty. Ltd. • 18/36 Ralph St. • Alexandria NSW 2015
Phone: 612-9669-4299 • Fax: 612-9669-4144 • www.hayhouse.com.au

*Published and distributed in the United Kingdom by:*
Hay House UK, Ltd. • 292B Kensal Rd., London W10 5BE
Phone: 44-20-8962-1230 • Fax: 44-20-8962-1239
www.hayhouse.co.uk

*Published and distributed in the Republic of South Africa by:*
Hay House SA (Pty), Ltd., P.O. Box 990, Witkoppen 2068
Phone/Fax: 27-11-467-8904 • info@hayhouse.co.za

*Published in India by:*
Hay House Publishers India, Muskaan Complex,
Plot No. 3, B-2, Vasant Kunj, New Delhi 110 070 • Phone: 91-11-4176-1620
Fax: 91-11-4176-1630 • www.hayhouse.co.in

*Distributed in Canada by:*
Raincoast • 9050 Shaughnessy St., Vancouver, B.C. V6P 6E5
Phone: (604) 323-7100 • Fax: (604) 323-2600 • www.raincoast.com

༄ ༄ ༄

**Take Your Soul on a Vacation**

Visit **www.HealYourLife.com®** to regroup, recharge, and
reconnect with your own magnificence. Featuring blogs, mind-body-spirit
news, and life-changing wisdom from Louise Hay and friends.

# HEAL YOUR LIFE ♥

## Take Your Soul on a Vacation

Get your daily dose of inspiration today at www.HealYourLife.com®.Brimming with all of the necessary elements to ease your mind and educate your soul, this Website will become the foundation from which you'll start each day. This essential site delivers the latest in mind, body, and spirit news and real-time content from your favorite Hay House authors.

## Make It Your Home Page Today!
### www.HealYourLife.com®

www.hayhouse.com®